# Introduction to Ethics

Introduction to Ethics

# Introduction to Ethics

Philosophy 240

3rd Edition

Jeff Kautz, MDiv

For Use with *Ethics for Life: A Text with Readings* 7th Edition by Judith Boss ISBN 978-1-259-91427-0
And Classroom and Blackboard Reading, Lecture, and Discussion

REVISED 3rd Edition December 2018

Printed in the United States of America

ISBN-13: 9781731010414



Redhawk Publishing
2550 Hwy 70 SE
Hickory NC 28602

www.cvcc.edu

bookstore.cvcc.edu

Sources for borrowed material in Works Cited

# Content

# NOTES

# Ethical Theory

# Why Study Ethics?

Why Be Moral?

_____

_____

_____

_____

Why Study Ethics

- Ethics are important because _____

  _____

  _____

- Ethics are crucial because

  _____

  _____

- Morality is primarily concerned with

  _____

  _____

  _____

Some related Questions

- What _____

- What _____

- What _____

- What _____

- These are fundamental to your world view

Applications

- _____

- _____

- _____

- _____

- _____

- _____

Key Terms

- **Ethics-**_____

- **Morality-**_____

- Ethics are also important because you face moral choices every day
- What moral choices do you think you face today?

_____

- Ethics provide the basis on which you make those decisions

Is it right or wrong
- Speeding
- Paying for food
- Coming to class on time
- Murder
- Paying bills
- Cheating
- Stealing
- Rape
- Helping the less fortunate
- Abortion
- Capital Punishment
- Suicide
- Euthanasia
- War
- Poverty
- Stem Cell Research
- Cloning

Ask yourself why do you want to study ethics?

_____

_____

_____

_____

_____

_____

_____

_____

_____

_____

_____

_____

_____

_____

_____

_____

_____

_____

_____

_____

_____

_____

_____

_____

_____

_____

| Ethical Theories vs. Applied Ethics | |
|---|---|
| • | • |
| • | • |
| • | • |
| • | • |
| • | • |
| • | • |
| • | • |
| • | • |

Broad Ethical Categories

- Descriptive Ethics

  _____

- Normative Ethics

  _____

- Metaethics

  _____

- Virtue Ethics

  _____

Clear Expectations

- Remember to listen when others are speaking
- Everyone has the right to their own opinion
- Strive to form a safe classroom environment
- Participate in class discussion
- Encourage one another and be a positive leader
- Challenge yourself to be the best that you can be
- Take responsibility for your actions

# NOTES

# Chapter 1 Ethics: An Overview

Ethics and Morality

- Ethics-_____

- Morality-_____

Three Parts of Morality

1. External

    _____

    _____

2. Internal

    _____

    _____

3. Serving

    _____

    _____

Moral Philosophy

- Three Parts Related Trends in Moral Philosophy

    ○ _____

    ○ _____

    ○ _____

- Philosophical ethics analyzes and evaluates these guidelines in light of accepted universal principles and concerns

Normative and Theoretical Ethics

- **Theoretical Ethics/Metaethics-**

  _____

- **Normative Ethics-**

  _____

Normative Ethics
- Affects our lives at all levels: _____

Metaethics Ethics
- The starting point is the most basic insights regarding morality

- _____

  _____

Metaethical Theories

| Non-cognitive | Cognitive | |
|---|---|---|
| Emotivism | <u>Relativist Theories</u><br>Ethical Subjectivism<br>Cultural Relativism<br>Divine Command | <u>Universalist Theories</u><br>Ethical Egoism<br>Utilitarianism<br>Natural Law Ethics<br>Deontology<br>Virtue Ethics<br>Rights Ethics |

Emotivism
- **Emotivism**

_____

_____


Relativist vs. Universalist
- Relativist

_____

- Universalist

_____

_____


Relativist Theories

- **Ethical Subjectivism-**

_____

_____

- **Cultural Relativism-**

_____

_____

- **Divine Command-**

_____

_____

Universalist Theories

- _____

- _____

- These principles exist independently of an individual's or a society's opinion

Metaphysics

- **Metaphysics-**

  _____

  _____

Metaphysical Dualism and Materialism

- Metaphysical Dualism-

  _____

- Metaphysical Materialism-

  _____

Determinism

- _____

- We are governed by unconscious forces

- _____

- Existentialist believe the opposite that we are defined by our freedom and we have the responsibility to create our own moral principles upon which we act

Moral Actions

- Categories of Moral Action

  ○ _____

    - May do or not do without incurring any moral guilt
    - Acts that are _neither_ mandated nor forbidden
    - Example: jogging 3 times a week
    - _____

      _____

      _____

      _____

      _____

      _____

      _____

      _____

  ○ _____

    - A deed that is _either_ mandated or prohibited
    - A mandate cannot be avoided without moral censure
    - A prohibition cannot be engaged without moral censure
    - Example: being faithful to your spouse, killing an innocent person
    - _____

      _____

      _____

      _____

      _____

      _____

      _____

      _____

- ○ _____
  - • An act that goes beyond the call of duty
  - • A deed that is morally praiseworthy but cannot be required
  - • Example: Jumping on a grenade to save others in platoon
  - • _____

    _____

    _____

    _____

    _____

    _____

    _____

    _____

    _____

How to Define the Nature of Ethical Norms

- • _____
  - ○ No universal norms of any sort
  - ○ Conflicting moral norms cannot arise
  - ○ Decisions made on personal grounds
  - ○ _____

    _____

    _____

    _____

    _____

    _____

    _____

    _____

    _____

- _____
  - No universal norms only general guidelines
  - Conflicting moral norms do not arise
  - General rules allow exceptions in specific cases as a way to resolve conflicts
  - _____

    _____

    _____

    _____

    _____

    _____

    _____

    _____

    _____

- _____
  - Only one universal norm (i.e. do the right thing)
  - The "right" thing varies from situation to situation
  - Conflicting norms cannot arise because of the overarching principle of the situation
  - _____

    _____

    _____

    _____

    _____

    _____

    _____

    _____

    _____

- _____
  - Many universal ethical norms
  - Ethical norms can and do conflict in some situations
  - May be forced to break a norm, but doing so always remains "wrong"
  - Example: Bonhoeffer's decision to take part in plot to assassinate Hitler. Murder is always wrong but is forgivable if necessary to prevent greater evil (the murder and torture of thousands of innocent Jews)
  - _____
    _____
    _____
    _____
    _____
    _____
    _____
    _____
    _____
    _____

- _____
  - Many universal ethical norms
  - Norms are arranged in a discernable hierarchy
  - Ethical norms can and do conflict from time to time
  - Not wrong to break a lower norm in order to keep a higher one
  - Example: Corrie ten Boom telling lie to Nazi to save Jews hiding in her home
  - The hierarchy of norms is not always clear and if the right course not obvious, then we must simply do the best we can to decide between conflicting duties
  - _____
    _____
    _____
    _____
    _____
    _____
    _____
    _____
    _____
    _____

- _____
  - This is based on recognizing that the Ten Commandments are all much more than simple rules
  - All succinctly state the unexceptional norm at the center of a distinctly separate category in God's moral revelation
  - The 9th commandment do not bear false witness the sanctity of truth states the unexceptional core of God's truth norm
  - We should not assume we know what "truth" means before learning what God says it means in the Bible
  - God's moral standards never conflict

  - _____

  _____

  _____

  _____

  _____

  _____

  _____

  _____

  _____

# NOTES

# Chapter 2 Critical Thinking and Moral Reasoning

Critical Thinking
- 3 Levels of Thinking
- Experience-

_____

_____

_____

_____

- Interpretation-

_____

_____

_____

_____

- Analysis-

_____

_____

_____

_____

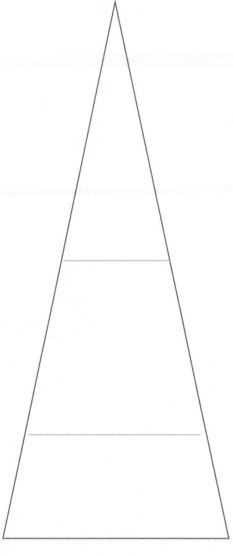

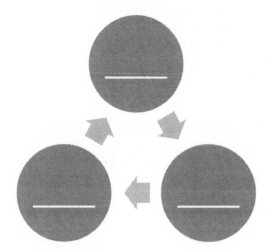

Overcoming Resistance

- Defense Mechanisms-

  _____

  _____

- Healthy Defense Mechanisms:

  - Coping-

    _____

    _____

- Immature Defense Mechanisms

    - Resistance—

    _____

    _____


    - Ignorance—

    _____

    _____


    - Avoidance—

    _____

    _____


    - Denial—

    _____

    _____


    - Anger—

    _____

    _____


    - Clichés—

    _____

    _____


    - Superficial Tolerance—

    _____

    _____

- "I'm Struggling"—

  _____

  _____

- Distractions—

  _____

  _____

- Doublethink—

  _____

  _____

## Descriptive vs. Prescriptive

- Descriptive Statements—

  _____

  _____

- Prescriptive Statements—

  _____

  _____

- Ethics

  _____

  _____

Constructing Moral Arguments

- Premise-

  _____

  _____

- Conclusion-

  _____

  _____

- Argument-

  _____

  _____

Two types of arguments

- Deductive-

  _____

  - All killing of unarmed people is morally wrong. Capital punishment involves
    the killing of unarmed people. Therefore, capital punishment is morally wrong
- Inductive-

  _____

  - Murder rates are not significantly lower in states that have capital punishment.
    Therefore, capital punishment is probably not an effective deterrent against
    murder.

## Breaking Down An Argument

- The entire argument may appear in either one sentence or several sentences
- The conclusion can appear anywhere in the argument
- Identify the conclusion first. Ask yourself: What is this person trying to prove?
- Look for keyword indicators **PLEASE SEE CHART PAGE 28.**
- Underline the conclusion and the premises

## Exercise

Every physician should cultivate lying as a fine art…Many experiences show that patients do not want the truth about their maladies, and that it is prejudicial to their well-being to know it

## Rhetoric And Moral Arguments

- Rhetoric—

  _____

  _____

- Five Steps to constructing a moral argument
    1. Develop a list of premises
    2. Eliminate irrelevant or weak premises
    3. Come to a conclusion
    4. Try out your argument on others
    5. Revise your argument if necessary

## Activity

1. No one under eighteen-years-old can vote. Jen is under eighteen-years-old. Therefore, Jen cannot vote.

2. A good society treasures its dissidents and mavericks because it needs the creative thinking that produces new hypotheses, expanded means, a larger set of alternatives, and, in general, the vigorous conversation induced by fresh ideas.

3. Since in American schools every child is unique and of equal worth with every other child, academic competition, which subverts this egalitarian and individualist creed, must be discouraged.

4.  With what group do I belong? I am with those who would be pleased to be refuted if I
    should say anything that is not true, and pleased to be the refuter of anyone who should
    say anything that is not true--more pleased, in fact, to be refuted than to refute. I think
    that's a greater good, you see, insofar as it's a greater good to be relieved of a great evil
    than to relieve another of the same.

## The Use of Evidence

- Personal Experience-

  _____

  _____

- Unpublished reports-

  _____

  _____

- Published reports-

  _____

  _____

- Eyewitness testimony-

  _____

  _____

- Celebrity testimony-

  _____

  _____

- Expert opinion-

  _____

  _____

- Experiment-

  _____

  _____

- Statistics-

  _____

  _____

- Survey-

  _____

  _____

- Formal observation-

  _____

  _____

- Research review-

  _____

  _____

## Fallacies

- Fallacy typically occur when we are unsure of our position
- Being able to identify and recognize fallacies makes us less likely to fall victim to them and to use them in an argument
- Fallacy of Equivocation—

  _____

  _____

  - Ex. Giving money to charity is the right thing to do. So charities have a right to our money
- Appeal to Force—

  _____

  _____

  - Ex. Don't disagree with me because of you do I'll slap you.
- Abusive Fallacy—also know as Ad Hominem—

  _____

  _____

  - Ex. Jane has written several books arguing that pornography harms women. Jane is a bitter and ugly person and you should not listen to her

- Appeal to Authority—also known as Inappropriate Authority—

  _____

  _____

  - Ex. Many actors have come out against capital punishment so we should do away with it
- Popular Appeal—Also known as Bandwagon, Ad Populum, Plain Folks—

  _____

  _____

  - Ex. Everyone else was cheating so that makes it okay
- Hasty Generalization—

  _____

  _____

  - Ex. All wealthy people are snobs or all blonds are dumb
- Ignorance—

  _____

  _____

  - Ex. For years people have been trying to prove that UFO's exist. But on one has yet to prove it. Therefore, they do not exist.
- Begging the question—

  _____

  _____

  - Ex. Voluntary euthanasia  is morally acceptable because people have the right to choose when and how they will end their lives
- Appeal to Tradition—

  _____

  _____

  - Ex. Slavery should remain legal, because that is the way it has always been

- Slippery Slope—

  _____

  _____

  - Ex. Animal experimentation reduces our respect for life. If we don't respect life, we are likely to me more tolerant of violent acts like war and murder
- Non-Sequitur—

  _____

  _____

  - Ex. I think I would make a good diplomat to China. I have a very good record in dealing with minorities.
- Either/Or—also known as False Dichotomy—

  _____

  _____

  - Ex. The PAAP building is in bad shape. Either we tear it down and put up a new building, or we continue to risk student's safety. Obliviously we shouldn't risk anyone's safety so we should tear it down.
- Red Herring—

  _____

  _____

  - Ex. A politician is asked a question about raising taxes but answers with information about the environment
- Strawman—

  _____

  _____

  - Ex. After Will said that we should put more money into health and education, Warren responded by saying that he was surprised that Will hates our country so much that he wants to leave it defenseless by cutting military spending.

- Appeal to Pity—

  _____

  _____

  - Ex. I know the exam is graded based on performance, but you should give me an A. My cat has been sick, my car broke down and I've had a cold, so it was really hard for me to study.
- False Clause—also know at Post Hoc—

  _____

  _____

  - Ex. President Jones raised taxes, and then the rate of violent crime went up. Jones is responsible for the rise in crime.

## Steps to Resolving a Moral Dilemma

- Moral dilemmas

- _____

- _____

- _____

- _____

- _____

- _____

| Premise Indicators | | Conclusion Indicators | |
|---|---|---|---|
| • Since<br>• Because<br>• For<br>• As<br>• Follows from<br>• As shown by<br>• Inasmuch as | • As indicated by<br>• The reason is that<br>• May be inferred from<br>• May be derived from<br>• May be deduced from<br>• Given that | • Therefore<br>• Hence<br>• So<br>• Accordingly<br>• Consequently<br>• Proves that<br>• As a result<br>• Thus | • For this reason<br>• For these reasons<br>• It follows that<br>• I conclude that<br>• Which shows that<br>• Which means that<br>• Which entails that<br>• Which implies that |

## Notes

_____

_____

_____

_____

_____

_____

_____

_____

_____

_____

_____

_____

_____

_____

_____

_____

_____

# Chapter 3 Moral Development and Conscience

- The study of ethics must take into account relevant facts about human nature and behavior
- The primary reason for studying ethics is to make us better people and we must understand the development and the process it plays

---

**SELF-EVALUTION QUESTIONNAIRE***

Jennifer, a college junior, is taking five courses and doing an internship while trying to maintain her 4.0 GPA so she can get into a good law school and become a civil rights lawyer. After staying up all night to complete a fifteen-page term paper, Jennifer realizes that she forgot to write a four-page response paper due for an English literature class she's taking. Strapped for time and not wanting to damage her grade in the course, she remembers another student in her class telling her about a Web site that sells essays. She goes to the Web site and finds an essay that fits the assignment. Should Jennifer buy the paper and turn it in as her own?

*Looking at the following list determine which considerations are most important to you in deciding what to do, with (1) being not important at all to (5) being very important.[3]*

| | | | | | |
|---|---|---|---|---|---|
| a) Whether the campus rules against plagiarism should be respected. | 1 | 2 | 3 | 4 | 5 |
| b) What is the risk that Jennifer will get caught? | 1 | 2 | 3 | 4 | 5 |
| c) Is it fair to the other students applying to law school if Jennifer isn't caught and gets accepted instead of them because she turned in a plagiarized essay? | 1 | 2 | 3 | 4 | 5 |
| d) Other students in the class are plagiarizing so why shouldn't Jennifer? | 1 | 2 | 3 | 4 | 5 |
| e) Will turning in the paper from the Internet be best for her future career? | 1 | 2 | 3 | 4 | 5 |
| f) Is she violating the rights of the professor and other students in the class by turning in the essay? | 1 | 2 | 3 | 4 | 5 |
| g) Did the professor bring this on himself by placing too many demands on his students? | 1 | 2 | 3 | 4 | 5 |
| h) Is there a way Jen can maintain her grade average without cheating and possibly lowering the grades of other students? | | | | | |

---

## What Is Conscience?

- Conscience-_____

- It provides _____

- It involves _____

- Conscience _____

- C.S. Lewis- "we must believe that conscience of man is not a product of nature"

- "Human beings, all over the earth, have this curious idea that they ought to behave in a certain way, and cannot really get rid of it"

- Plato defined conscience as an activity of the soul that directs us toward the good.

- _____

  _____

  Plato even suggested for the execution of these people or those "whose souls are incurably evil."

## Three Factors To Conscience

1. _____

2. _____

3. _____

## Heredity and Biological Factors

- Altruistic Behavior-

  _____

  _____

- _____

## Learning or Environmental Factors

- _____

  _____

  _____

## Determinism vs. Moral Responsibility

- Determinism

  _____

  _____

- Moral Responsibility--

  _____

  _____

## Affective and Cognitive Side Of Conscience

- Conscience can be broken into two parts

  - Affective—

    _____

- Cognitive

  _____

  _____

- Moral knowledge

  _____

  _____

  _____

- Moral sentiments

  _____

  _____

  _____

- Sympathy

  _____

  _____

  _____

- Moral Outrage

  _____

  _____

  _____

- Moral indignation—

  _____

  _____

  _____

- Guilt

_____

_____

_____

## The Stage Theory of Moral Development

### TABLE 3.1    Kohlberg's Stages of Moral Development

| STAGE | DESCRIPTION |
|---|---|
| **Preconventional** | |
| 1. Punishment and obedience | Avoid punishment; submit to authority. Fear of punishment is the primary motive. |
| 2. Egoist | Satisfy one's own needs; only consider the needs of others if it benefits you: "You scratch my back, I'll scratch yours." |
| **Conventional** | |
| 3. Good boy/nice girl | Please and help others; concern for maintaining good relationships and earning others' approval; conformity to peer and group norms. |
| 4. Society maintaining | Respect authority and social rules; maintain the existing social order. |
| **Postconventional** | |
| 5. Social contract or legalistic | Obey useful, albeit arbitrary, social rules; appeal to social consensus and majority rule as long as minimal basic rights are safeguarded. The U.S. Constitution is written using this stage of reasoning. |
| 6. Conscience and universal principles | Autonomously recognize universal rules, such as justice and equality, that are rational and logically consistent and reflect a respect for equal human rights and the dignity of each individual. |

## Moral Behavior

"There is widespread agreement that there are more components to morality than just moral judgment. The trick, however, is to identify what else there is in morality and how all these pieces fit together." James Rest, p. 99

## Four Components Of Moral Behavior

- Moral Sensitivity-

  _____

  _____

- Moral Reasoning or Judgment-

  _____

  _____

- Moral Motivation-

  _____

  _____

- Moral Character-

  _____

  _____

## NOTES

# Chapter 4 Ethical Subjectivism

- Morality is a private choice—Craig Price (convicted serial killer)
- "Take any vicious action...willful murder, for instance.  Examine it in all lights, and see if you can find that matter of fact, or real existence, which you call vice...you can never find it, till you turn your reflection into your own breast, and find a sentiment of disapproval, which arises in you, toward this action.  Here is a mater of fact, but 'tis the object of feeling, not reason."
David Hume


- **Ethical Subjectivism-**

  _____

  _____


- Sometimes called

  _____


- This means that people can never be mistaken about what is morally right or wrong

  because there are no objective or universal moral standards or truths only opinions

- **Opinion-**

  _____

  _____


Problem

- People have different opinions, but were morality is concerned, there are no

  _____ and no one is _____. People just feel differently

  about things and that's all there is to it.

- Ethical Subjectivism

  _____

  _____

- According to this theory there is no such thing as

_____

## What Ethical Subjectivism Is Not

- Tolerance

_____

_____

_____

- Ethical Skepticism

_____

_____

_____

- Emotivism

_____

_____

_____

# Notes_____

_____

_____

_____

_____

_____

_____

_____

_____

# Summary of Three Ethical Theories

|  | Ethical Skepticism | Emotivism | Ethical Subjectivism |
|---|---|---|---|
| Agreement on a set of *objective* standards for resolving moral differences |  |  |  |
| Convincing Evidence for Objective standards? |  |  |  |
| Moral Statements Are? |  |  |  |
| Truth-Value? |  |  |  |
| Truths Based Upon? |  |  |  |
| Conclusion |  |  |  |

The Kitty Genovese Syndrome

- Ethical theories

  _____

- They are to inform and motivate our

  _____

- Values Clarification

  _____

  _____

- Nihilism

  _____

  _____

A Critique

1. _____

   _____

   _____

   _____

2. _____

   _____

   _____

   _____

3. _____

   _____

   _____

   _____

4. _____

   _____

_____

_____

### Conclusion

Moral thinking and moral conduct are a matter of weighing reasons and being guided by them. But being guided by reason is very different from following one's feelings. When we have strong feelings, we may be tempted to ignore reason and go with the feelings. But in doing so, we would be opting out of moral thinking altogether. This is why, in focusing on attitudes and feelings, Ethical Subjectivism seems to be going in the wrong direction.

# Notes_____

_____

_____

_____

_____

_____

_____

_____

_____

_____

_____

_____

_____

_____

_____

_____

_____

_____

_____

_____

_____

_____

_____

# Chapter 5 Divine Command Theory

- "The Good consists in always doing what God wills at any particular moment." Emil Brunner, *The Divine Imperative* (1947)
- "The heart has its reasons which reason does not know. . . . It is the heart which experiences God, and not the reason. " Blaise Pascal, *Penees*

Two Advantages

1. _____

   _____

2. _____

   _____


- Religion—

   _____

   _____


- The concept of God in Judaism, Christianity and Islam is so intimately connected to

   the concept

   _____

   _____


- Divine Command-

   _____

   _____

- Civil Religion-

  _____

  _____

- Natural Law-

  _____

  _____

## Euthyphro

- Plato, "do the gods love holiness because it is holy or is it holy because the gods love it"
- "Is conduct right because the gods command it, or do the gods command it because it is right"
- "God makes the moral truths true or does He merely recognize their truth"
- _____

  _____

## Key Claims of Divine Command

- _____

  _____

- _____

  _____

- _____

  _____

## Critiques Of Divine Command

- _____

  _____

- _____

  _____

- _____

  _____

## Civil Religion

- Civil religion claims that morality, at least to some extent, is relative to a particular culture or nation
- The primary role of civil religion is the creation of a sense of cultural or national identity and purpose
- Civil Religion_____

  _____

  _____

## Does Morality Need Religion

- C. S. Lewis said: _"If no set of moral ideas were better than another, there would be no sense in preferring civilized morality to Nazi morality. The moment you say one lot of morals is better than another, you are in fact measuring them by an ultimate standard."_

- _____

  _____

## Spirituality vs. Religious

- Religious-

  _____

  _____

- Spirituality-

  _____

  _____

# NOTES

# Chapter 6 Cultural Relativism

- Morality differs in every society, and is a convenient term for socially approved habits—Ruth Benedict, *Patterns of Culture (1934)*
- Herodotus said that conceptions of right and wrong differ from culture to culture

- Cultural Relativism-

_____

_____

_____

- _____

_____

_____

- _____

_____

_____

- _____

_____

_____

## What Cultural Relativism Is Not

- Excusing

_____

_____

_____

- Respect for Cultural Diversity

_____

_____

_____

## Cultural Relativism vs. Sociological Relativism

- Cultural Relativism

_____

_____

- Sociological Relativism

_____

_____

## Cultural Difference Argument

- The Eskimos saw nothing wrong with _____, whereas Americans believe

  that _____ is immoral.

- Therefore infanticide is neither _____. It is merely a

  matter of opinion, which _____.

- _____

  _____

- Therefore, there is no _____.

_____

_____

Claims By Cultural Relativists

1. _____

   _____

   _____

2. _____

   _____

   _____

3. _____

   _____

   _____

4. _____

   _____

   _____

5. _____

   _____

   _____

Critiques

1. _____

   _____

   _____

   _____

2. _____

_____

_____

3. _____

_____

_____

_____

4. _____

_____

_____

_____

5. _____

_____

_____

_____

6. _____

_____

_____

_____

7. _____

_____

_____

_____

# NOTES

# Chapter 7 Ethical Egoism

Three Types of Ethical Egoism

1. Individual Ethical Egoism

   _____

   _____

2. Personal Ethical Egoism

   _____

   _____

3. Universal Ethical Egoism

   _____

   _____

- Ethical Egoism

   _____

   _____

- Ethical subjectivism is about

   _____

- Ethical egoism is concerned

   _____

Key Claims

- _____

   _____

- _____

  _____

- _____

  _____

## Egoism vs. Hedonism

- Hedonism is a doctrine that considers

  _____

  _____

## Psychological Egoism

- Psychological Egoism seizes on the fact that we are in part motivated by

  _____

  _____

- Psychological Egoism makes a claim about

  _____

- Ethical Egoism makes a claim about

  _____

## Ayn Rand

- Believe in Ethical Egoism
- She believed that we can best create an atmosphere where each individual can pursue his or her own interest by protecting people's individual liberty rights
- That we value that which helps us survive and that which helps us survive is what is in our own self-interest
- She believed that we are fundamentally solitary individuals, each pursuing our own self-interest
- Self-interested people help others only if they will get something in return.

## Arguments for Ethical Egoism

There are at least three principal arguments in support of ethical egoism:

1. _____

2. _____

3. _____


1. _____

_____

_____

2. _____

- Ethical egoists sometimes maintain that if each person took care of himself/herself, the overall effect would be to make the world a better place for everyone.

- *Epistemological:* _____

- *Moral:* _____

- Reply: this justification ultimately appeals to utilitarian principles, not the principles of ethical egoism.

3. _____

- This argument presupposes the people in fact already act selfishly (i.e, psychological egoism) and are just pretending to be altruistic.
- If psychological egoism is true, then we should admit its truth and get rid of our hypocrisy.
- Reply: it may not make a big difference in a world of independent adults, but in a world with children and people at risk or in need, they would be put in further jeopardy.

## Criticisms of Ethical Egoism

1. _____

2. _____

3. _____

4. _____


1. _____
   - Can the ethical egoist consistently will that everyone else follow the tenets of ethical egoism?
   - It seems to be in one's self-interest to be selfish oneself and yet get everyone else to act altruistically (especially if they act for your benefit). This leads to individual ethical egoism.
   - Some philosophers such as Jesse Kalin have argued that in sports we consistently universalize ethical egoism: we intend to win, but we want our opponents to try as hard as they can!

2. _____
   - Some philosophers have argued that ethical egoism is, at best, appropriate to living in a world of strangers that you do not care about.

3. _____

   - _____
   - If friendship involves (among other things) being concerned about other people for their own sake, then this seems something beyond the reach of the egoist.
   - Ethical egoists can help their friends if they believe there is a long-term payoff for doing so.

4. _____
   - Can the ethical egoist be sensitive to the suffering of others?
   - Such sensitivity seems to presuppose caring about other people for their own sake.
   - Moral sensitivity presupposes that the suffering of others exerts a moral "pull" on the individual—something that the ethical egoist does not recognize.

The Truths in Ethical Egoism

- Sometimes self-interest masquerades as altruism
- Ethics should not deny the importance of self-interest
- Self-love is a virtue, but it is not the only virtue Ethical egoism mistakes a part of the picture for the whole picture

# Chapter 9 Natural Law

- At its basic understanding, moral or natural law is grounded in rational human nature

- **Natural Law**

  _____

  _____

- Morality is

  _____

  _____

- Reason helps to keep our emotions and/or passions in check

- Natural law is **teleological**—

  _____

  _____

## Four Arguments for the Existence of God

- Cosmological—

  _____

  _____

  _____

- Teleological—

  _____

  _____

  _____

- Ontological—

_____

_____

_____

- Moral Law Argument—

_____

_____

_____

- The goal for humans is *eudaimonia* or happiness

- The four fundamental goods are

_____

- An action is right if it brings about or promotes one of these fundamental goods
- The basic principle is to "do good and avoid evil"

Human Laws

- Aquinas wrote: "Human law has the aspect of law to the extent to which it is in accord with the correct norm, and from this viewpoint it is evidently derived form the eternal law."

- Human laws are only binding

_____

- We cannot take refuge in

_____

- Christian and Jewish natural law look toward a day, in the messianic age, when human law will be in perfect harmony with natural law

Natural Law Ethics and Religion

- Natural law

  _____

  _____

- Natural law

  _____

  _____

- Natural law

  _____

  _____

## Key Claims of Divine Command

1. _____

   _____

2. _____

   _____

3. _____

   _____

4. _____

   _____

Four Types of Law

- Eternal Law-

  _____

  _____

- Divine Law-

  _____

  _____

- Natural (Moral) Law-

  _____

  _____

- Human Law-

  _____

  _____

Civil Disobedience

- Civil disobedience-the refusal on moral grounds to obey certain government laws for the purpose of trying to bring about a change in legislation or government policy
- When laws may be unjust

1. _____

2. _____

3. _____

4. _____

Criteria for Civil Disobedience

1. _____

2. _____

3. _____

4. _____

Critique of Natural Law

1. _____

_____

2. _____

_____

3. _____

_____

4. _____

_____

5. _____

_____

# NOTES_____

_____

_____

_____

_____

_____

# Chapter 12 Virtue Ethics

Virtue Ethics and Character

- **Virtue Ethics**

  _____

- Virtue Ethics are character based ethics

- Virtue Ethics

  _____

  _____

- Virtue

  _____

  _____

- 4 cardinal or natural virtues:

  _____

  _____

History of Virtue Ethics

- Aristotle-(4th Century BC)

  _____

  _____

  - He asks "what is the good of man?" and answers with "an activity of the soul in

    conformity with virtue"

- Early Christianity

  _____

  _____

- Greeks

  _____

  _____

- Augustine-(4ᵗʰ Century AD)

  _____

  _____

- Renaissance period-(1400-1650)

  _____

  _____

- Elizabeth Anscombe-(1958)—*Modern Moral Philosophy*

  _____

  _____

## What Are Virtues?

- Virtues are an

  _____

  _____

- Confucianism—*jen*

  _____

  _____

- Hinduism

  _____

- Christianity

  _____

- A trait of character,

  _____

- Moral Virtues—Intellectual vs. Moral

| | | |
|---|---|---|
| | | |
| | | |
| | | |
| | | |
| | | |
| | | |
| | | |
| | | |

Virtue vs. Vice

- A virtue is the midpoint between two extremes the vice of excess and the vice of deficiency

- Vice

  _____

  _____

- Vices stand in our way of achieving happiness and the good life

Virtue Advantages

- _____

  _____

- _____

  _____

- _____

  _____

- _____

  _____

- _____

  _____

- _____

  _____

# Applied Ethics

# Abortion

## 5 Basic Questions That Frame Any Approach To Bioethics

1. _____

2. _____

3. _____

4. _____

5. _____

## Four Principles of Bioethics

1. Autonomy—

   _____

   _____

2. Beneficence—

   _____

   _____

3. Justice—

   _____

   _____

   _____

4. Nonmaleficence—

_____

_____

## Abortion

### General Statistics

- The _____ most common surgical procedure

- Since, Roe v. Wade in 1973, abortions have risen from 775,000 to 1.6 million annually

- That is about _____ pregnancies

### Legal History

- _____

  - Essentially stopped the government's ability to stop abortion
  - Even late pregnancy abortions cannot be prohibited if doctor certifies that abortion is necessary to preserve the mother's health
  - Divided pregnancy into "trimesters"
  - First Trimester: _____

    - States can make _____ regulations regarding abortion

  - Second Trimester: _____

    - States may choose to regulate abortion procedures in ways related to maternal health

    - States still can make _____ regulations with respect to the fetus

  - Third Trimester: _____

    - Looks like it permits states to protect fetus after "viability" but renders it virtually impossible
    - Says, "the State...may, if it chooses, regulate, and even prohibit abortion except where it is necessary, in appropriate medical judgment, for the preservation of the life or health of the mother"

- _____

  - Determined "mother's health" should be interpreted the broadest possible way
  - Said interpretation could include psychological, emotional, and family-related
  - But all pregnancies affect a woman's mental state, emotions and family relationships
  - So, Doe v. Bolton offers legal cover for abortion on demand to the last day of a pregnancy

- _____

  - Prohibited states from requiring a father's consent
  - Prohibited states from requiring parents of a pregnant minor to consent
  - Prohibited states from outlaw the saline solution technique in second trimester abortions
  - Gave physicians great latitude on choosing what to do with an undesired baby who
  - is born alive during an abortion procedure

- _____

  - Shifted focus of abortion regulation to the state level
  - Allowed (but did not require states to:
    - Prohibit public employees from performing abortions except to save mother's life
    - Refuse public funding for abortion counseling
    - Prohibit public officials from encouraging abortion if not necessary to save mother's life
    - Mandate tests to determine viability of baby more than 20 weeks old

- _____

  - A ban outlawing the procedure was signed into law by President Bush on November 5, 2003

**Key Terms**

**Types of Abortions**

- Spontaneous

  _____

  _____

- Induced

  _____

  _____

  - Therapeutic

    _____

    _____

  - Eugenic

    _____

    _____

  - Elective

    _____

    _____

- Zygote

  _____

  _____

- Embryo

  _____

  _____

- Fetus

  _____

  _____

- Viability

  _____

  _____

Notes_____

_____

_____

_____

_____

_____

_____

_____

_____

_____

_____

_____

When Does Human Life Begin

❖ _____ View

- A person evolves over time

- Personhood is achieved in social interaction, does not begin at conception

- Not full person until fully capable of social interaction

- Must achieve criteria such as: conscious thought, aware of things external to self, able to feel pain, able to reason, capable of self-motivated activity

- Objections

    - Bases personhood on arbitrary stipulations, so who chooses

    - If one can choose any set of stipulations, then any category of human life can be excluded

    - Arguments would justify euthanasia, genocide, killing the handicapped

    - Could ignore the poor, sick, uneducated, because they are less of a person

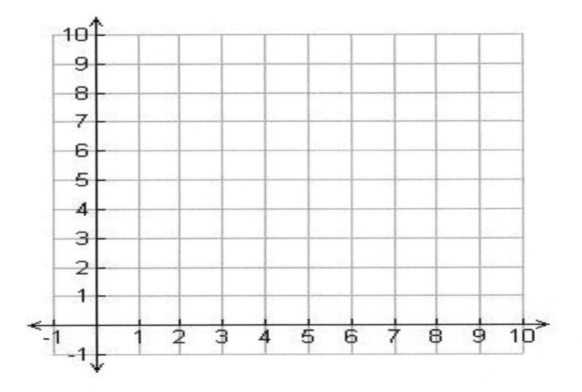

❖ _____ View

- Personhood is fundamentally linked to the biological presence of human life

- Personhood is the essential aspect of human life

- Emphasizes species-specific DNA is present at fertilization

- Personhood begins at conception

- Objections

  - Seems to make the value of persons depend on chemical values

  - If persons are souls, this would mean large number of souls are never born

  - Identical twins usually do not split until second week

Techniques of Abortion

➢ _____

- Used about 20 % of $1^{st}$ trimester abortions

- The cervix is dilated and the uterine wall is scraped

➢ _____

- Used for about 80% of $1^{st}$ trimester abortions

- The cervix is dilated and a suction tube is inserted into womb

- The suction tears the fetus from the womb

➢ _____

- Most common for $2^{nd}$ trimester abortions

- Needle is inserted into the amniotic sac and some fluid is removed and replaced with a concentrated salt solution

- The fetus is slowly poisoned

➤ _____

- Most common for 3rd trimester abortions

- Same procedure as cesarean but with different outcomes

- Physician is permitted great latitude if the fetus remains alive after being taken from the womb

**Arguments For Abortion**

1. _____

   _____

2. _____

   _____

3. _____

   _____

4. _____

   _____

5. _____

   _____

## Arguments Against Abortion

1. _____

   _____

2. _____

   _____

3. _____

   _____

4. _____

   _____

5. _____

   _____

6. _____

   _____

## Rape and Incest

- This is a debate between both sides
- Both sides recognize the seriousness and brutality and violence of rape and incest crimes
- Both sides want to seek to help the victims and punish the criminals
- **Arguments to permit for rape or incest**

  - _____

    _____

  - _____

    _____

- ▪ _____

  _____

- Arguments against permitting for rape or incest

  - ▪ _____

    _____

  - ▪ _____

    _____

  - ▪ _____

    _____

- **What You Should Know About Partial-Birth Abortion**

- **What is partial-birth abortion?**
- Under federal-law, "partial-birth abortion" means an abortion in which the person performing the abortion deliberately and intentionally vaginally delivers a living fetus until, in the case of a head-first presentation, the entire fetal head is outside the body of the mother, or, in the case of breech presentation, any part of the fetal trunk past the navel is outside the body of the mother, for the purpose of performing an overt act that the person knows will kill the partially delivered living fetus and performs the overt act, other than completion of delivery, that kills the partially delivered living fetus.[1]

- **Is partial-birth abortion legal?**
- No, there is currently a federal ban on the procedure.  A partial birth abortion ban was passed twice in Congress in the late 1990s, but President Bill Clinton vetoed both bills.  Another version was signed into law in 2003 by President George W. Bush.

- In 2004, Planned Parenthood Federation of America and other abortion groups challenged the law and three federal district courts ruled the ban unconstitutional.  In 2007, the Supreme Court heard this case, _Gonzales v. Carhart_, and ruled in a 5-4 decision that the ban was constitutional.

---

[1] Jeffrey, Terence. "AG Nominee Defending Partial-Birth Abortion: 'The Phrase "Living Fetus"' is 'Hopelessly Vague'." http://www.cnsnews.com/news/article/terence-p-jeffrey/ag-nominee-defending-partial-birth-abortion-phrase-living-fetus. (accessed May 26, 2017)

- Additionally, <u>19 states have their own bans</u> on partial-birth abortion.

- **Isn't the term partial-birth abortion a political term, rather than a medical one?**
- The term partial-birth abortion is a non-medical term used colloquially, like heart attack or stroke, to refer to a medical-related condition or action. (A more accurate term would be partial-delivery abortion.) The term refers to the procedure known as intact dilation and evacuation (D&E) or dilation and extraction (D&X).

- The term partial-birth abortion was coined in 1995 by Florida Congressman Charles T. Canady who introduced the first Partial-Birth Abortion Ban Act in Congress.

- **Why not use the medical term rather than the political term?**
- The American College of Obstetricians and Gynecologists defines dilation and evacuation (D&E) as a "surgical procedure in which the cervix is dilated and the contents of the uterus are removed." This procedure could describe both the removal of the fetus after a miscarriage or the partial delivery of a fetus for the purpose of abortion. The term partial-birth abortion is preferable because it provides a clear and necessary distinction between the morally neutral actions in which the D&E procedure may be performed and the use of the technique for the purposes of infanticide.

- **Why is partial-birth abortion so often referred to as infanticide?**
- Almost every state in the U.S. uses the same standard for reporting a live birth: 'Live Birth' means the complete expulsion or extraction from its mother of a product of human conception, irrespective of the duration of pregnancy, which, after such expulsion or extraction, breathes, or shows any other evidence of life such as beating of the heart, pulsation of the umbilical cord, or definite movement of voluntary muscles, whether or not the umbilical cord has been cut or the placenta is attached. Heartbeats are to be distinguished from transient cardiac contractions; respirations are to be distinguished from fleeting respiratory efforts or gasps.[2]

- By leaving a part of the body in the womb, the abortionist is able to avoid the legal criteria of "complete expulsion or extraction from the mother." This allows them to kill the child without violating the law protecting children after a live birth. This legal loophole, however, does not change the fact that the procedure is a form of infanticide: the act of killing an infant, a child during the earliest period of its life.

- **How many partial-birth abortions were performed before the federal ban was implemented?**
- According to the <u>Guttmacher Institute,</u> the research arm of Planned Parenthood, an estimated total of thirty-one providers performed partial-birth abortions 2,220 times in 2000.

---

[2] Commonwealth Law Revision Commission. http://www.cnmilaw.org/pdf/cmc_section/T1/26005.pdf. (accessed May 26, 2017).

- In Ramesh Ponnuru's book *The Party of Death*, one source commented on this figure that, "If a new virus were killing 2,200 premature babies in neonatal units, it would be on the TV evening news every week."

- **Why doesn't the partial-birth abortion ban take account of the life and health of the mother?**
- The federal partial-birth abortion ban does not prohibit physicians from performing the procedure if necessary to "save the life of the mother whose life was endangered by a physical disorder, physical illness, or physical injury, including a life-endangering physical condition caused by or arising from the pregnancy itself."[3]

- The "health" exception, however, is legally broad that when applied it cannot be used to prevent any abortions. In the landmark Supreme Court case *Doe v. Bolton*, Justice Harry Blackmun wrote, The medical judgment may be exercised in the light of all factors—physical, emotional, psychological, familial and the woman's age—relevant to the well-being of the patient. All these factors may relate to health. This allows the attending physician the room he needs to make his best medical judgment. And it is room that operates for the benefit, not the disadvantage of the pregnant woman.[4]

- What this means is that the health exception can be used almost any time the woman or the doctor chooses. This is why the effect of *Doe* was established abortion on demand throughout the entire nine months of pregnancy. If a doctor is willing to do the procedure and claims that a woman's "emotional health" is at risk, a healthy child could legally be aborted the day the woman goes into labor.

- Pro-abortion politicians often refer to the "health exception" because it would, following Judge Blackmun's reasoning, allow them to prevent any abortion restrictions throughout the pregnancy.

---

[3] Partial-Birth Abortion: Recent Developments in the Law.
http://congressionalresearch.com/RL30415/document.php?study=Partial-Birth+Abortion+Recent+Developments+in+the+Law. (accessed May 26, 2017).
[4] Doris Gordon. "Abortion and Rights: Applying Libertarian Principles Correctly." *The International Journal of Sociology and Social Policy* 19, no. 3 (1999): 96-126.

# Just War Theory

Key Terms

- Pacifism-

  _____

  _____

  - Three Types of Pacifism

    1) Absolute Pacifists—

       _____

       _____

    2) Satyapraha—

       _____

       _____

    3) Conscientious Objection—

       _____

       _____

- Crusade-

  _____

  _____

- Just War-

  _____

  _____

Characteristics of Just War Theory

1. _____

_____

2. _____

_____

3. _____

_____

4. _____

_____

5. _____

_____

6. _____

_____

7. _____

_____

8. _____

_____

Just War Theory

*Jus ad bellum*—conditions that should be met before going to war

1.  Competent Authority--

    _____

    _____

2.  Just Cause--

    _____

    _____

3.  Right Intent—

    _____

    _____

4.  Last Resort--

    _____

    _____

5.  Probability of Success--

    _____

    _____

6.  Proportionality of Projected Results--

    _____

    _____

7.  Right Spirit—

    _____

    _____

*Jus in bello*—conditions that should be met for a war to be conducted justly

1.  <u>Discrimination</u>--

_____

_____

2.  <u>Proportionality In Use of Force</u>--

_____

_____

3.  <u>Proportionality of Projected Results</u>—

_____

_____

4.  <u>Right Spirit</u>--

_____

_____

# NOTES

Thomas Aquinas, *Summa Theologica*, Part II, Question 40
Of War... First Article

Whether It Is Always Sinful To Wage War

In order for a war to be just, three things are necessary. First, the authority of the sovereign by whose command the war is to be waged. For it is not the business of a private individual to declare war, because he can seek for redress of his rights from the tribunal of his superior. [...] And as the care of the common weal is committed to those who are in authority, it is their business to watch over the common weal of the city, kingdom or province subject to them. And just as it is lawful for them to have recourse to the sword in defending that common weal against internal disturbances, when they punish evil -doers, according to the words of the Apostle (Romans 13:4): "*He beareth not the sword in vain: for he is God's minister, an avenger to execute wrath upon him that doth evil*"; so too, it is their business to have recourse to the sword of war in defending the common weal against external enemies. Hence it is said to those who are in authority (Psalm 81:4): "*Rescue the poor: and deliver the needy out of the hand of the sinner*"; and for this reason Augustine says (Contra Faust. xxii, 75): "*The natural order conducive to peace among mortals demands that the power to declare and counsel war should be in the hands of those who hold the supreme authority.*"

Secondly, a just cause is required, namely that those who are attacked, should be attacked because they deserve it on account of some fault. Wherefore Augustine says (QQ. in Hept., qu. x, super Jos.): "*A just war is wont to be described as one that avenges wrongs, when a nation or state has to be punished, for refusing to make amends for the wrongs inflicted by its subjects, or to restore what it has seized unjustly.*"

Thirdly, it is necessary that the belligerents should have a rightful intention, so that they intend the advancement of good, or the avoidance of evil. Hence Augustine says (De Verb. Dom. [The words quoted are to be found not in St. Augustine's works, but Can. Apud. Caus. xxiii, qu. 1): "*True religion looks upon as peaceful those wars that are waged not for motives of aggrandizement, or cruelty, but with the object of securing peace, of punishing evil-doers, and of uplifting the good.*" For it may happen that the war is declared by the legitimate authority, and for a just cause, and yet be rendered unlawful through a wicked intention. Hence Augustine says (Contra Faust. xxii, 74): "*The passion for inflicting harm, the cruel thirst for vengeance, an unpacific and relentless spirit, the fever of revolt, the lust of power, and such like things, all these are rightly condemned in war.*"

# Capital Punishment

Statistics

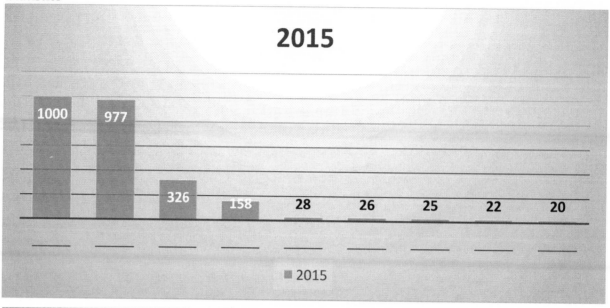

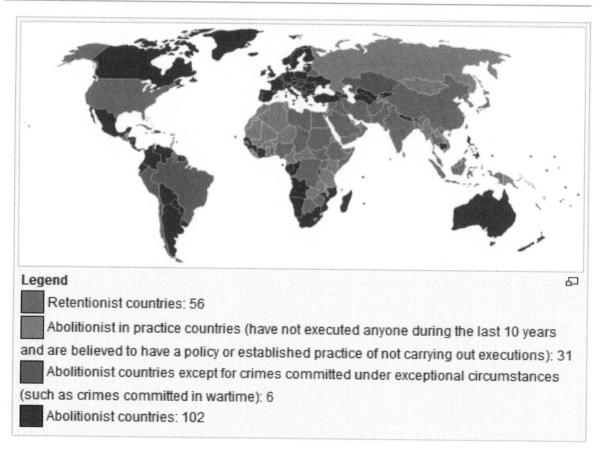

**Legend**

Retentionist countries: 56

Abolitionist in practice countries (have not executed anyone during the last 10 years and are believed to have a policy or established practice of not carrying out executions): 31

Abolitionist countries except for crimes committed under exceptional circumstances (such as crimes committed in wartime): 6

Abolitionist countries: 102

## Death Penalty States

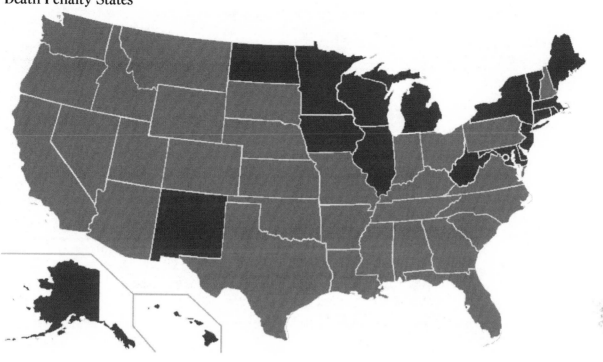

| State | Since 1977 | Last | Murder Rate |
|-------|-----------|------|-------------|
|       |           |      |             |
|       |           |      |             |
|       |           |      |             |

## RACE OF DEFENDANTS EXECUTED

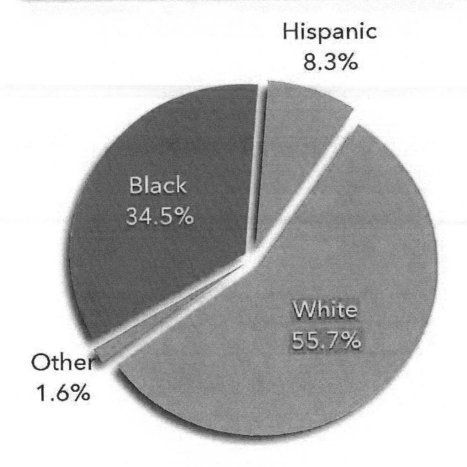

- White: 801
- Black: 496
- Hispanic: 119
- Other: 23

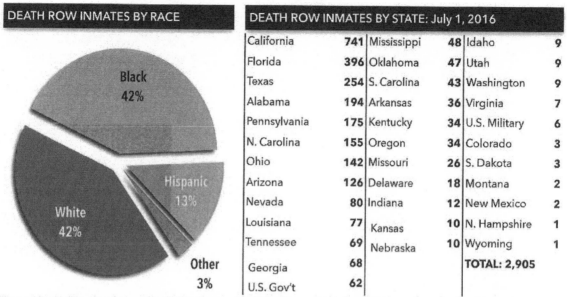

**Race of Death Row Inmates** and **Death Row Inmates by State** Source: NAACP Legal Defense Fund, "Death Row USA" (July 1, 2016). When added, the total number of death row inmates by state is slightly higher than the given total because some prisoners are sentenced to death in more than one state.

What the Death Penalty Is

- Capital Punishment—death penalty—

  _____

  _____

  _____

  _____

- Two Court Cases

  1. _____

     _____

  2. _____

     _____

Three Perspectives on Capital Punishment

- Abolitionist

  _____

  _____

  _____

- Retentionists

  _____

  _____

  _____

- Procedural Abolitionists

  _____

  _____

  _____

Justifications of Punishment

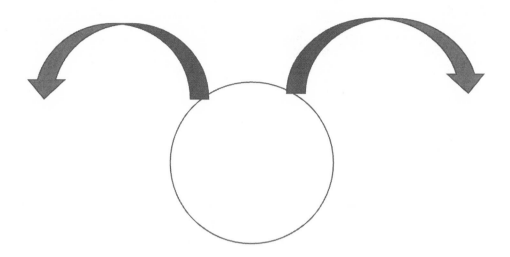

- Recall two ways of justifying punishment
    - Backward-looking:

      _____

      _____

    - Forward-looking:

      _____

      _____


Retributivism

- *Lex talionis,* "an eye for an eye," "a tooth for a tooth"
- Core concept:

  _____

  _____


Is Retributivism Just Revenge?

- Critics of retributivism

_____

_____

➢ Replies:

- Yes, it is revenge, but that's ok
- No, retribution is about something more than revenge: about balancing the scales of justice, about safeguarding the rights of victims, and about changing perpetrators.
-

The Scales of Justice

➢ Fundamental metaphor: an underlying balance which must, if upset, be put back in order

➢ Punishment is

_____

_____

The Rights of Victims
- ➢ Victims, some retributivists argue, have a right to see the perpetrators suffer their just desserts
  - Example: families of victims at executions

The Effects on Perpetrators
- ➢ Some retributivists, argue that punishment should have certain effects on the perpetrators, including
  - insight into their crime, including compassion for victim
  - will "wipe the slate clean"

Criticisms of Retributivism

- ➢ _____

  _____

- ➢ _____

  _____

- ➢ _____

  _____

Changes to the Death Penalty In North Carolina

- • _____

  _____

- • _____

  _____

- • _____

  _____

- • _____

  _____

## North Carolina Degrees of Felony Homicide

- _____
  _____
- _____
  _____
- _____
  _____

## Deterrence

- ➤ Many justify punishment as an institution by its deterrent effect
- ➤

  - • Specific deterrence:

    - • _____
      _____

  - • General deterrence:

    _____
    _____

## Normative and Empirical Considerations

- ➤ The deterrence argument has two premises:

- ➤ Empirical Premise: _____

- ➤ Normative Premise: _____

- ➤ Conclusion: _____

## Empirical Premise: Punishment deters crime.

- ➤ Un-controversially true in general sense, but does it deter those who are worst criminals?
- ➤ Are other means of deterrence better?

➤ It is important to realize that, for most people,

_____

_____:

- _____

- _____

- _____

- _____

- _____

## Punishment and Prevention

➤ Overall goal: _____

➤ Punishment is _____

➤ Preventive approaches
➤ Current approaches:
- Surveillance
- Predictive policing

## Rehabilitation

➤ _____

_____

➤ _____

_____

➤ _____

_____

➤ _____

_____

Arguments Against Capital Punishment

1. _____

_____

2. _____

_____

3. _____

_____

4. _____

_____

5. _____

_____

6. _____

_____

Arguments For Capital Punishment

1. _____

_____

2. _____

_____

3. _____

_____

4. _____

_____

# NOTES

# Stem-Cell Research

## Background

- Use of stem cells began in the _____ with the use of _____, given by mouth for treatment of _____

- The first real _____ of stem cells came in the late _____

- The possibilities of using stem cells for research and treatment of a variety of diseases generated a lot of excitement

- Both public and private funding of research regarding stem cells for curing degenerative diseases has been progressing

- In _____ allowed the first federally funded study using embryonic stem cells

- Bush allowed for studies using _____ and the federal projects should not encourage the _____

- Critics claimed that limiting embryonic stem cells research to "_____" did not offer sufficient "_____" for reliable research

- In 2006 Bush vetoed "_____" that would have allowed for the use of excess frozen _____

- In 2009 _____ rescinded the ban

- Currently scientists at _____ have found stem cells in amniotic fluid that is showing promise

## Facts About Stem Cells

- Human stem cells are cells that have not yet received instructions on what function they should grow to support—all their genetic switches are still in the ON position
- They are undifferentiated, self-replicating cells with the potential to become any of the differentiated cells that make up the various tissues in the human body
- Two categories (more or less)

    ➢ _____

    ➢ _____

- **Adult Stem Cells**

    _____

    _____

- **Embryonic Stem Cells**

    _____

    _____

    _____

    _____

## Stem Cell by "potency"

- _____-These are cells that

    "_____" They are also

    called "conceptual" stem cells because they only exist at the point "conception" and

    initial cell division

- _____-these are cells that

    "_____" These may also

be called "embryonic" stem cells because they come from cells that have started to differentiate in the second stage of early development called a "blastocyst"

- _____-These cells that

  "_____" These cells come from life developing in the womb after the "blastocyst" stage, and they are called "adult" stem cells because they have already become so specifically coded and they can only become one of two or three different things and nothing else.

- _____-these are cells that

  "_____" They are stem cells in the sense of being available to "replace" other damaged cells. But all genetic codes in these cells have been turned off except for one and a "unipotent" cell will only turn into that one thing.


- Embryonic Stem Cells must be taken at the blastocyst stage happens between 5-6 days after fertilization


- Adult Stem cells can be harvested from different sources:

  - _____

  - _____

  - _____

  - _____

  - _____

  - _____

  - _____

## Advances Have Been Made Using Adult Stem Cells

- A U.S. biochemical firm inserted anti-HIV genes into human stem cells, which grew into the type of white blood cell HIV infection destroys, showing potential for treatment that reverses the effects of HIV
- Stem cell therapies will never cure Alzheimer's because stem cell treatment only has potential for curing degenerative diseases or for growing replacement organs and Alzheimer's is a whole brain disease

## Misconceptions

- It is widely argued that embryonic stem cell researchers is the gold standard of stem cell research, and that they have more promises than adult stem cells. But in reality is that ALL progress in stem cell research to-date has been achieved with adult stem cells.

# NOTES

_____

_____

_____

_____

_____

_____

_____

_____

_____

_____

_____

_____

_____

_____

_____

_____

# Euthanasia

- Euthanasia—_____

- It covers a range of practices involving if or when it would be moral to

_____, by _____, either the timing or

methodology of _____, or both, when doing so might

_____ or

_____


Terms of Distinction

- Voluntary/Involuntary Euthanasia:

  _____

  _____

- Active/Passive Euthanasia:

  _____

  _____

- Direct/Indirect Euthanasia:

  _____

  _____

Giving an incompetent person, such as an infant or person in a coma a lethal injection

Physician-assisted suicide; administering a lethal injection or lethal dose at a patient's request

Withholding life support or medical treatment from an incompetent person

Withholding life support or medical treatment at the patient's direct request or indirectly through a living will

Terms

- **Allowing Someone to Die—**

  _____

  _____

  _____

  _____

- **Mercy Death—**

  _____

  _____

- **Mercy Killing—**

  _____

  _____

Legal History

- Currently _____ states prohibit mercy death and make it illegal under homicide statutes

- All but _____ states outlaw mercy death

- Brain Death—_____

- Four criteria-

  1. _____

     _____

  2. _____

     _____

  3. _____

     _____

  4. _____

     _____

- Persistent Vegetative State (PVS)-

- _____

- Three Cases Surrounding PVS

  1. Karen Ann Quinlan

     _____

     _____

  2. Nancy Cruzan

_____

_____

3. Terri Schiavo

_____

_____

## Advanced Directives

- Protect our autonomy
- Durable Power of Attorney for Health Care

_____

_____

- Can state what measures should or should not be taken to keep them alive

## Physician Assisted Suicide

- PAS

_____

_____

- Dr. Jack Kevorkian—_____, 1990

  helped Janet Adkins, who was in the early stages of Alzheimer's, end her life.

- Legal in:

_____

Requirements for PAS

- _____

  _____

- _____

  _____

- _____

  _____

- _____

  _____

- _____

  _____

- _____

  _____

Hospice Care

- Started in _____ to help people die

  with dignity rather than with fear

- First Hospice care in the US _____

- Primary role is to provide palliative care—

  _____

- Hospice opposes the legalization of euthanasia

## Arguments in Favor of Euthanasia

1. _____

_____

2. _____

_____

3. _____

_____

4. _____

_____

## Arguments Used Against Euthanasia

1. _____

_____

2. _____

_____

3. _____

_____

# NOTES

Tips taken from Mr. Collie at CVCC

Remembering the following tips, when writing a research paper, can make one or two letter grade difference in the final paper!

- No contractions – Contractions are not incorrect grammar, but they characterize a more casual writing style than scholars strive for.
- No numeric expressions for values that can be expressed in three words or less.  Some writing experts suggest writing out all numbers of one hundred or below and using numeric expressions for values above one hundred – ask instructor if unsure.  Write out all numbers in word format less than 100.  Ex.  Fifty-five not 55, 1.2 million is okay, 1 million should be one million, 5% should be five percent.
- NEVER begin a sentence with a numeric expression.
- Avoid abbreviations in heading, title, or body of paper as they do not lend themselves well to a formal academic paper.
- Acronyms are fine—provided the full term is shown at first mention, with the acronym following in parentheses. For example, "I work at Catawba Valley Community College, (CVCC)."  After this sentence, it is perfectly acceptable to merely use the acronym for future references.
- Avoid slang words or expressions – for example, rather than saying something was growing "like weeds," you might say, "burgeoning" or "expanding exponentially."  Instead of something being "a killer achievement," you might say it was "significant."  The goal is not to try to use words beyond your vocabulary, but to sound professional—not casual or slang.
- Write at college level—high school student researchers often use phrases like, "this paper will explain how . . ." or "Now, I am going to show how . . ."  While this is not grammatically incorrect, it has an elementary sound to it.  Because college prepares students for the professional world, students should begin to write with a more professional look and sound.  The writer/researcher becomes more confident and trustworthy—in the readers' mind—by just making the points directly; there is no need to tell the reader that you are about to make a point—just make it.
- Always capitalize the FIRST and LAST word in the title of an academic paper.
- In a Turabian style paper, EVERY source used should be in the Works Cited page and EVERY source listed in the Works Cited page should be cited in a footnote in the body of the paper
- Capitalize proper nouns, and italicize published titles and works.
- The first paragraph must contain a clear thesis statement – the topic of your paper and some of the highlights of your findings.  This not only tells the readers what to expect from the paper, but it makes your job—as the writer—easier by establishing a framework that the remaining paragraphs will build upon.  Just as every sentence in a paragraph relates to the main idea of the paragraph, every paragraph should relate to the thesis in some way.
- No new information should be presented in the final paragraph. The last paragraph is critical, nonetheless, as it reiterates the thesis (not in the exact words) and concludes and summarizes the paper.

- If a book is assigned with this project, a single theme or concept from the book should dominate the paper. In other words, while the book is just one of a number of sources—all of the other sources are selected because they relate to the chosen theme from the book, which is your main source. While there is no set number of times you should reference the book, I would expect it to be mentioned and cited numerous times throughout the paper; one of the characters or themes should be prominent in the research paper.

- Paper appearance should remain consistent throughout—do not change font styles or size in the paper; this is often a problem when students copy and paste quotes from outside sources. Be sure to modify the font to the required Times New Roman, 12 point. See that margins, spacing, and indentions remain consistent, as well.

- If an Internet source has a URL longer than two lines, please reduce its length by copying and pasting it in the provided space at: tinyurl.com. In a matter of seconds, this website tool will generate a short, working URL to replace the long one. Use this new short URL for listing in your Works Cited or References page.

# Turabian Style Citations (Notes-Bibliography Style)

This guide provides basic guidelines and examples for citing sources using *A Manual for Writers of Research Papers, Theses, and Dissertations*, 7th edition, by Kate L. Turabian.

Turabian style includes two options for citing sources: the notes-bibliography style and the author- date style. This guide covers the notes-bibliography style for writers who are using endnotes or footnotes as a means of giving attribution to their sources.

## Books

| Book: One Author | **Format for Citation:**<br>Author Last, First. *Title*. Location of Publisher: Publisher, Year of Pub.<br><br>**Format for Note:**<br>Note number. Author First Last, *Title* (Location of Publisher: Publisher, Year of Pub.), pages cited.<br><br>**Sample Citation:**<br>Welch, Kathleen E. *Electric Rhetoric: Classical Rhetoric, Oralism and a New Literacy*. Cambridge: MIT Press, 1999.<br><br>**Sample Note:**<br>43. Kathleen E. Welch, *Electric Rhetoric: Classical Rhetoric, Oralism and a New Literacy* (Cambridge: MIT Press, 1999), 143. |
|---|---|

Citation and Bibliography

Kautz, Jeff. *PHI 240: Introduction to Ethics*. Hickory: Redhawk Publications, 2017. Revised May 2018.

Footnote

Note Number, Jeff Kautz, *PHI-240: Introduction to Ethics*. (Hickory: Redhawk Publications, 2018). Page Cited.

| | |
|---|---|
| **Book: Two or More Authors** | **Format for Citation:**<br>Author Last, First, and Author First Last. *Title*. Location of Publisher: Publisher, Year of Pub.<br><br>**Format for Note:**<br>Note number. Author First Last and Author First Last, *Title* (Location of Publisher: Publisher, Year of Pub), pages cited.<br><br>[Note: Include all authors regardless of number in the order they appear on the book's title page when creating your Bibliography. Abbreviated author entries are allowed in endnotes or footnotes, using the terms "et al." or "and others." See page 163 in *A Manual for Writers of Term Papers, Theses, and Dissertations* by Kate L. Turabian for further information.]<br><br>**Sample Citation:**<br>Lunsford, Andrea, and Lisa Ede. *Singular Texts/Plural Authors: Perspectives on Collaborative Writing*. Carbondale: Southern Illinois University Press, 1990.<br><br>Patten, Michael A., Guy McCaskie, and Philip Unitt. *Birds of the Salton Sea: Status, Biogeography, and Ecology*. Berkeley: University of California Press, 2003. |
| | **Sample Note:**<br>8. Andrea Lunsford and Lisa Ede, *Singular Texts/Plural Authors: Perspectives on Collaborative Writing* (Carbondale: Southern Illinois University Press, 1990), 59-60.<br><br>11. Michael A. Patten, Guy McCaskie, and Philip Unitt, *Birds of the Salton Sea: Status, Biogeography, and Ecology* (Berkeley: University of California Press, 2003), 52. |
| **Electronic Book** | **Format for Citation:**<br>Author Last, First. *Title*. Location of Publisher: Publisher, Year of Pub. Format of e-book.<br><br>**Format for Note:**<br>Note number. Author First Last, *Title* (Location of Publisher: Publisher, Year of Publication), format of e-book.<br><br>**Sample Citation:**<br>Welch, Kathleen E. *Electric Rhetoric: Classical Rhetoric, Oralism and a New Literacy*. Cambridge: MIT Press, 1999. netLibrary e-book.<br><br>**Sample Note:**<br>15. Kathleen E. Welch, *Electric Rhetoric: Classical Rhetoric, Oralism and a New Literacy* (Cambridge: MIT Press, 1999), netLibrary e-book. |

| | |
|---|---|
| **Chapter in a Book** | **Format for Citation:**<br>Author Last, First. "Title of Chapter/Article." In *Title*, edited by First Name Last, Inclusive page numbers. Location of Publisher: Publisher, Year of Publication.<br><br>**Format for Note:**<br>    Note number. Author First Last, "Title of Chapter/Article," in Title, ed. Editor's First Last Name (Location of Publisher: Publisher, Year of Pub.), pages cited.<br><br>**Sample Citation:**<br>Wells, Ida B. "Lynch Law in All Its Phases." In *With Pen and Voice: A critical anthology of nineteenth-century African-American women*, edited by Shirley Wilson Logan, 80-99. Carbondale: Southern Illinois University Press, 1995.<br><br>**Sample Note:**<br>    32. Ida B. Wells, "Lynch Law in All Its Phases," in *With Pen and Voice: A critical anthology of nineteenth-century African-American women*, ed. Shirley Wilson Logan (Carbondale: Southern Illinois University Press, 1995), 34. |
| **Translated Book** | **Format for Citation:**<br>Original Author Last, First. *Title*. Translated by First Name Last. Location of Publisher: Publisher, Year of Publication.<br><br>**Format for Note:**<br>    Note number. Original Author First Last, *Title*, trans. First Name Last (Location of Publisher: Publisher, Year of Pub.), pages cited.<br><br>**Sample Citation:**<br>Eisenstein, Sergei. *Film Sense*. Translated by Jay Leyda. London: Faber and Faber, 1968. |
| | **Sample Note:**<br>    23. Sergei Eisenstein, *Film Sense*, trans. Jay Leyda (London: Faber and Faber, 1968), 14-15. |

Journals

| | |
|---|---|
| **Journal Article: Print** | **Format for Citation:**<br>Author Last, First. "Title." *Journal Name* volume #, no. issue # (Month/Season Year): inclusive page numbers.<br><br>**Format for Note:**<br>Note number. Author First Last, "Title," *Journal Name* volume #, no. issue number (Month/Season Year): page number used.<br><br>**Sample Citation:**<br>Haraway, Donna J. "A Game of Cat's Cradle: Science Studies, Feminist Theory, Cultural Studies." *Configurations* 2, no. 1 (1994): 59-71.<br><br>**Sample Note:**<br>33. Donna J. Haraway, "A Game of Cat's Cradle: Science Studies, Feminist Theory, Cultural Studies," *Configurations* 2, no. 1 (1994): 64. |
| **Journal Article:**<br><br>**Two or More Authors** | **Format for Citation:**<br>Author Last, First, and Author First Last. "Title." *Journal Name* volume #, no. issue # (Day Month Year): inclusive page numbers.<br><br>**Format for Note:**<br>Note number. Author First Last and Author First Last, "Title," *Journal Name* volume #, no. issue number (Month/Season Year): page number used.<br><br>[Note: Include all authors regardless of number in the order they appear in the byline for the article. Abbreviated author entries are allowed in endnotes/footnotes, using "et al." or "and others." See page 163 of the Turabian manual for more information.]<br><br>**Sample Citation:**<br>Gautreau, Ronald, and Jeffrey M. Cohen. "Birth and Death of a Black Hole." *American Journal of Physics* 65 (May 1997): 444-446.<br><br>**Sample Note:**<br>14. Ronald Gautreau and Jeffrey M. Cohen, "Bird and Death of a Black Hole," |
| **Journal Article:**<br><br>**From a Full-Text Database** | **Format for Citation:**<br>Author Last, First. "Title." *Journal Name* volume #, no. issue # (Month or Season Year): inclusive page numbers if available. URL (accessed Month Day, Year).<br><br>**Format for Note:**<br>Note number. Author First Last, "Title," *Journal Name* volume #, no. issue # (Month or Season Year): page numbers used, URL (accessed date of access). |

| | |
|---|---|
| | **Sample Citation:**<br>Ferrell, Robert H. "Truman's Place in History." *Reviews in American History* 18, no. 1 (March 1990): 1-9. http://www.jstor.org/stable/2702718 (accessed February 3, 2005).<br><br>**Sample Note:**<br>14. Robert H. Ferrell, "Truman's Place in History," *Reviews in American History* 18, no. 1 (March 1990): 8-9, http://www.jstor.org/stable/2702718 (accessed February 3, 2005). |
| Journal Article: Online | **Format for Citation:**<br>Author Last, First. "Title." *Journal Name* volume #, issue # (Month Day, Year of Pub), URL (accessed Month Day, Year of Access).<br><br>**Format for Note:**<br>Note number. Author First Last, "Title," *Journal Name* volume #, issue # (Month Day, Year of Pub), URL (accessed Month Day, Year of Access).<br><br>**Sample Citation:**<br>Jobe, Karen D. "Women and the Language of Hackerdom: The Gendered Nature of Hacker Jargon." *Kairos* 5, no. 2 (Fall 2000), http://english.ttu.edu/kairos/5.2/binder.html?coverbweb/jobe/women&hackerdom.htm (accessed March 23, 2005).<br><br>**Sample Note:**<br>42. Karen D. Jobe, "Women and the Language of Hackerdom: The Gendered Nature of Hacker Jargon," *Kairos* 5, no. 2 (Fall 2000), http://english.ttu.edu/kairos/5.2/binder.html?coverweb/jobe/women&hackerdom.htm (accessed 23 March 2005). |

Magazines

| | |
|---|---|
| Magazine Article: Print | **Format for Citation:**<br>Author Last, First. "Title." *Magazine Name*, Month Day, Year.<br><br>**Format for Notes:**<br>    Note number. Author First Last, "Title," *Magazine Name*, Month Day, Year, page number used.<br><br>[Note: Bibliographic citations do not require inclusive page numbers for an article, although these may be included. Page numbers cited should be included in the note.]<br><br>**Sample Citation:**<br>Swartz, Mimi. "An Enron Yard Sale." *New Yorker*, May 6, 2002.<br><br>**Sample Note:**<br>    13. Mimi Swartz, "An Enron Yard Sale," *New Yorker*, May 6, 2002, 51. |
| Magazine Article:<br><br>Two or More Authors | **Format for Citation:**<br>Author Last, First, and Author First Last. "Title." *Magazine Name*, Month Day, Year.<br><br>**Format for Notes:**<br>    Note number. Author First Last and Author First Last, "Title," *Magazine Name*, Month Day, Year, pages used.<br><br>[Note: For more information on citing more than two authors, see the explanation under "Journal Article: Two or More Authors."]<br><br>**Sample Citation:**<br>Silver, Marc, and James M. Pethokoukis. "Attack of the Cloned Light Sabers." *U.S. News & World Report*, May 13, 2002.<br><br>**Sample Note:**<br>    41. Marc Silver and James M. Pethokoukis, "Attack of the Cloned Light Sabers," *U.S. News & World Report*, May 13, 2002, 63. |

| | |
|---|---|
| Magazine Article: from a Full-Text Database | **Format for Citation:**<br>Author Last, First. "Title." *Magazine Name*, Month Day, Year. URL<br>    (accessed Month Day, Year).<br><br>**Format for Notes:**<br>    Note number. Author First Last, "Title," *Magazine Name*, Month, Day, Year of Pub, pages used, URL (accessed Month Day, Year).<br><br>**Sample Citation:**<br>Swartz, Mimi. "An Enron Yard Sale." *New Yorker*, May 6, 2002.<br>    http://web.lexis-nexis.com/universe/document?_m=b68471eb6243cfc<br>    730dc18cc03d6c746&_docnum=1&wchp=dGLbVtb-<br>    zSkVA&_md5= 0c8c5465eafe026db72b1a417350c8e9 (accessed<br>    June 23, 2004).<br><br>**Sample Note:**<br>    13. Mimi Swartz, "An Enron Yard Sale," *New Yorker*, May 6, 2002, 51,<br>http://web.lexis-nexis.com/universe/document?_m=b68471eb6243cfc730dc18cc<br>03d6c746&_docnum=1&wchp=dGLbVtb-zSkVA&_md5=0c8c5465eafe026<br>db72b1a417350c8e9 (accessed June 23, 2004). |
| Magazine Article: Online | **Format for Citation:**<br>Author Last, First. "Title." *Magazine Name*, Month Day, Year of Pub.<br>    URL (accessed Month Day, Year of Access).<br><br>**Format for Notes:**<br>    Note number. Author First Last, "Title," *Magazine Name*, Month Day,<br>Year of Pub, URL (accessed Month Day, Year of Access).<br><br>**Sample Citation:**<br>Leonard, Andrew. "Embracing the Dark Side of the Brand." *Salon.com*, May 18,<br>    2005. http://www.salon.com/mwt/feature/2005/05/18/star_wars_lego/index_<br>    np.html (accessed May 22, 2005).<br><br>**Sample Note:**<br>    24. Andrew Leonard, "Embracing the Dark Site of the Brand," *Salon.com*,<br>May 18, 2005, http://dir.salon.com/story/mwt/feature/2005/05/18/star_wars_lego/<br>index.html (accessed May 22, 2005). |

## Newspapers

When using Turabian notes style, newspaper articles do not need to be included in the Bibliography, but they should be included as notes. For more information on citing newspaper items, see Kate L. Turabian's A Manual for Writers, 7th ed. p. 186-188.

| | |
|---|---|
| **Newspaper Article:**<br><br>Print | **Format for Notes:**<br>    Note number. Author First Last, "Title," *Newspaper Name*, edition info if necessary, Month Day, Year of Publication.<br><br>**Sample Note:**<br>    7. Tamar Lewin, "SAT essay scores are in, but will they be used?," *New York Times*, May 15, 2005. |
| **Newspaper Article:**<br><br>from a Full-Text Database | **Format for Notes:**<br>    Note number. Author First Last, "Title of Article," *Newspaper Name*, Month Day, Year of Publication, edition if necessary, URL (accessed Month Day, Year).<br><br>**Sample Note:**<br>    13. Matt Flores, "San Antonio, Texas-Area Business Students Manage Real Portfolio," *San Antonio Express-News*, December 18, 2001, http://find.galegroup.com/ itx/infomark.do?&contentSet=IACDocuments&type=retrieve&tabID=T004&prodId=SPN. SP00&docId=CJ120721119&source=gale&srcprod=SP00&userGroupName= txshracd2584&version=1.0 (accessed February 10, 2004). |
| **Newspaper Article:**<br><br>Online | **Format for Notes:**<br>    Note number. Author First Last, "Article Title," *Newspaper Name*, Month Day, Year of Publication, URL (accessed Month Day, Year).<br><br>**Sample Note:**<br>    19. Lynda V. Mapes, "Unearthing Tse-whit-zen," *Seattle Times*, May 25, 2005, http://seattletimes.nwsource.com/news/local/klallam/index.html (accessed August 1, 2005). |
| **Letter to the Editor** | **Format for Notes:**<br>    Note number. Author First Last, letter to the editor, *Newspaper Name*, Month Day, Year of Publication.<br><br>**Sample Note:**<br>    22. Deborah D. Davies, letter to the editor, *San Francisco Chronicle*, May 16, 2005. |

Electronic Sources

| | |
|---|---|
| **Multi-Page Internet Site:**<br><br>Entire Site | **Format for Citation:**<br>Last Name, First of Author. Title. URL (accessed Month Day, Year).<br><br>**Format for Notes:**<br>    Note number.  Last Name, First of Author, Title, URL (accessed Month Day, Year).<br><br>**Sample Citation:** |
| | Weissmann, Anne. Ernest Haeckel: Art Forms in Nature. http://www. mblwhoilibrary.org/haeckel/index.html (accessed January 14, 2007).<br>**Sample Note:**<br>    16. Anne Weissmann, Ernest Haeckel: Art Forms in Nature, http://www. mblwhoilibrary.org/haeckel/index.html (accessed January 14, 2007). |
| **Multi-Page Internet Site:**<br><br>Single Page on Site | **Format for Citation:**<br>Corporate Author Name or Last Name, First of Author. "Title of Page." Title of site. URL (accessed Month Day, Year).<br><br>**Format for Notes:**<br>    Note number. Corporate Author Name or Last Name, First of Author, "Title of Page," Title of site, URL (accessed Month Day, Year).<br><br>**Sample Citation:**<br>Sun, Yee-Fan. "Shacking Up." DigsMagazine. http://www.digsmagazine.com/ lounge/lounge_shackingup.htm (accessed March 2, 2005).<br><br>**Sample Note:**<br>    12. Yee-Fan Sun, "Shacking Up," DigsMagazine.com, http://www. digsmagazine.com/lounge/lounge_shackingup.htm (accessed March 2, 2005). |
| **Multi-Page Internet Site:**<br><br>Corporate Author | **Format for Citation:**<br>Corporate Author Name. Title of Site. Owner of site if different from author. URL (accessed Month Day, Year).<br><br>**Format for Notes:**<br>    Note number. Corporate Author Name, Title of Site, Owner of site if different from author, URL (accessed Month Day, Year).<br><br>**Sample Citation:**<br>Miller Center of Public Affairs. American President. University of Virginia. http://www.americanpresident.com (accessed June 14, 2005).<br><br>**Sample Note:**<br>    19. Miller Center of Public Affairs, American President, University of Virginia, http://www.americanpresident.com (accessed June 14, 2005). |

| | |
|---|---|
| Personal Home Page | **Format for Citation:**<br>Author Last, First. Title of home page. URL (accessed Month Day, Year).<br><br>**Format for Notes:**<br>    Note number. Author First Last, Title of home page, URL (accessed Month Day, Year).<br><br>**Sample Citation:**<br>Harvey, Billy. Billy Harvey Has Had Hair Longer Than Yours.<br>    http://www.billyharvey.com (accessed May 25, 2005).<br><br>**Sample Note:**<br>    18. Billy Harvey, Billy Harvey Has Had Hair Longer Than Yours, http://www.billyharvey.com (accessed May 25, 2005). |
| E-mail | **Format for Notes:**<br>    Note number. Author of e-mail, email message to author, Month Day, Year of email message.<br><br>**Sample Note:** |
| |     15. Christopher Nolan, e-mail message to author, September 5, 2003. |

Citing A Lecture Format
for Citation:
Last Name, First Name. "Presentation title." Presentation Type, Event from Sponsor, City, Date Conducted
Example:
Kautz, Jeff. "Presentation Title." Class Lecture, Catawba Valley Community College, Hickory, Date.
Format for Note:
Note Number First Name Last Name. "Presentation title." Presentation Type, Event from Sponsor, City, Date Conducted

# NOTES_____

# How To Format Your Research Paper Using Turabian Style

Format

- 1" margin on all sides
- Times New Roman, 12 pt. font
- Double spaced

Steps and directions are for Microsoft Word (Word for MAC will be a little bit different)

Page Numbers

- Page Number should be in the upper right hand corner starting on the first page.
- Go to Insert
- Choose Page Number, Top of Page, Plain Number 3

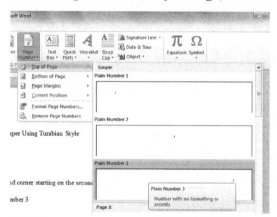

Click on Page Number and go to format page number, select start at and enter 0

- When page number appears, choose different first page. This will remove the page number from the first page. NO PAGE NUMBER SHOULD APPEAR ON THE FIRST PAGE.

## Title Page

- Go to the **Home** tab and click the **Center** button (or press Ctrl + E).
- Press the Enter key 4 times to place the cursor 2" from the top of the page. (Look at the ruler on the left. The cursor needs to be on or near the 1" mark. This will be 2" from the top because you've already added a 1" top margin).
- Type the <u>name of the college</u>.
- Press Enter 4 times.
- Type the <u>title of the paper</u>.
- Press Enter 4 times.
- Type the following lines, **pressing "Enter" once after each one:**
  - A Paper Presented to
  - Name of the professor
  - In Partial Fulfillment of the Requirements for the Course
  - Name of the course
- Press Enter 4 more times.
- Type your name and press "Enter" twice.
- Type the submission date in the following format: May 11, 2018
- Press Enter.

There is a sample cover page on page 113 or on the course Blackboard site

## Inserting A Footnote

- A footnote should be inserting a thought, idea, or quote that can be attributed to a source (book, journal article, newspaper, website, speech, etc.).
- All footnotes will appear at the bottom of the page they appear on.
- No parenthetical citations are to be used in Turabian style format.
- Your entries in the footnotes will be used to create your works cited page.

- All footnotes are to be placed at the end of a sentence after the period.[5]

- To insert a footnote

    - Click on Reference

    - Click on Insert Footnote

    - A number will appear; each new footnote will create a consecutive number.

    - That same number will appear at the bottom of the page. Type in your information following the guide given to you. **Note there is a difference in formatting between your footnotes and your works cited.**

    - When you are ready to insert your next footnote repeat the process.[6]

- TIPS

    - Once you have inserted footnote information for a resource you do not have to reinsert all the information over again. You can simply put the author's name and the page number.

    - If preceding footnote is from the same source simple use the word <u>Ibid</u> and the page number.

## Works Cited Page

- This page will be a listing of all the sources used in your paper. If you did not use a source in your paper, it should not be listed.

- The works cited page will come at the end of your paper and start on a new page.

- At the top of the new page type "Works Cited". This should be centered on the page, then return twice and start your listing of your sources.

---

[5] Footnote section
[6] Next footnote

- They should be in ABC order by author's last name. Follow the formatting given to you.**Set the Hanging Indents and Line Spacing for the Bibliography.** The Bibliography is typed so that the first line of each entry is even with the left margin, and all other lines are indented ½ inch. This format is known as a **hanging indent**. Each item is also single-spaced with a blank line separating one item from the next. Follow these steps to have Word do this automatically:

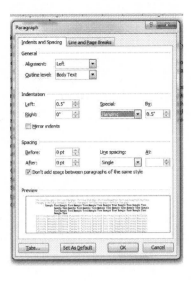

- On the **Home** tab or the **Page Layout** tab, locate the **Paragraph** group and click the small square that's located to the right of the word "Paragraph" (shown at the top of page 2).

- Click the **Indents and Spacing** tab if necessary.

- Set "**Special**" to **Hanging**.

- Set **Line Spacing** to **Single**.

- Click **OK**

(Formatted Cover Page)

Catawba Valley Community College

Title of Paper

A Paper Presented To:

Rev. Jeff Kautz

In Partial Fulfillment of the Requirements for the course

PHI 240-Introduction to Ethics

Your Name

Date

# Tests and Quizzes

Name: _____

# Les Misérables By Victor Hugo

| Main Characters: | |
|---|---|
| Jean Valjean (main character) | Inspector Javert |
| Cossette | Maris |
| The Bishop | The Housekeeper for Valjean |
| The Gardener (whose life Jean Valjean saved) | The prostitute woman (Cossette's mother) |

1) What do think the quote at the beginning of the movie means?

2) Do you think Jean Valjean was right to steal the bread?

3) What view did Inspector Javert have on the relation of law and morality?

4) What view did Jean Valjean have of law and morality?

5) How did Jean Valjean and Javert each view justice?

6) What did Jean Valjean and Javert each think of mercy?

7) How did the bishop affect justice by refusing to press charges against Jean Valjean?

8) Why did the bishop and Jean Valjean value mercy, and why could Inspector Javert never allow mercy? What made the difference?

9) Do you think Valjean let go of the rope on purpose or accident? If on purpose, do you think he helped that man so he could escape?

10) What led Jean Valjean's housekeeper (a former nun) to lie? When do you think she lied? Was it moral or immoral for her to lie? What did Jean Valjean think of her lie? What led Inspector Javert to refuse to believe she could ever lie?

11) The three times that Valjean helped save someone was witnessed by Javert. Why do you think Valjean did that while Javert did not?

12) While in prison Valjean says, "I'll kill you" to Javert.  Later he has the opportunity why does he not do it?

13) In deciding to commit suicide, what issue did Inspector Javert have to face?  What choices did he have, and what choice did he make?

14) The title of Victor Hugo's story is *Les Miserable*, which means "the miserable ones" or "the destitute."  Who in the story was "miserable" or "destitute"?

# Building A Better Argument
Directions: Underline the conclusion

1. "Since pain is a state of consciousness, a 'mental event,' it can never be directly observed." (source: Peter Singer, "Animal Liberation," 1973)

2. "All segregation statutes are unjust because segregation distorts the soul and damages the personality." (source: Martin Luther King Jr., "Letter from Birmingham Jail," 1963)

3. "Genes and proteins are discovered, not invented. Inventions are patentable, discoveries are not. Thus protein patents are intrinsically flawed." (source: Daniel Alroy, "Invention vs. Discovery," *The New York Times*, March 29, 2000)

4. A meter is longer than a yard. Therefore, since this ship is 100 meters long, it is longer than a football field.

5. "I hate books. They only teach us to talk about what we do not know." (source: Jean-Jacques Rousseau, "Emile," 1762)

6. "At any cost, we must have filters on our Ypsilanti Township library computers. Pornography is a scourge on society at every level. Our public library must not be used to channel this filth to the people of the area. (source: Rob J. and Joan D. Pelkey, letter to the editor, "The Ann Arbor News," February 3, 2004)

7. "Democracy has at least one merit, namely, that a member of Parliament cannot be stupider than his constituents, for the more stupid he is, the more stupid they were to elect him." (source: Bertrand Russell, "Autobiography," 1967)

8. "Twenty-eight children in the United States were killed by falling television sets between 1990 and 1997. That is four times as many people as were killed by great white shark attacks in the twentieth century. Loosely speaking, this means that watching 'Jaws' on TV is more dangerous than swimming in the Pacific. (source: "The Statistical Shark," *The New York Times*, September 6, 2001)

9. "It is a capital mistake to theorize before one has data. Insensibly one begins to twist facts to suit theories, instead of theories to suit facts." (source: Sherlock Holmes in Arthur Conan Doyle's "A Scandal in Bohemia," 1891)

10. "I think [Sen. John Kerry] was right [to vote against the Defense of Marriage Act]. I think he was right because what happened with the Defense of Marriage Act is it took away the power of states, like Vermont, to be able to do what they chose to do about civil unions, about these kinds of marriage issues.... I think these are decisions the states should have the power to make. And the Defense of Marriage Act, as I understand it...would have taken away that power. And I think that's wrong – that power should not be taken away from the states." (source: Sen. John Edwards, January 22, 2004

# Fallacies Activities

1. Voters are flocking to candidate R by the millions, so you'd better cast your vote the right way.

   _____

2. Betty Crocker is a hysterical feminist. We shouldn't listen to her views on sexual harassment.

   _____

3. Cam Newton says to use T-Mobile because that phone company is the best.

   _____

4. The TV news provides accurate and reliable information which was demonstrated conclusively on last week's 60 Minutes.

   _____

5. We should not rebuild the house because every time that we do, a tornado comes along and damages it.

   _____

6. If we can land on the Moon and Mars, then we can cure all diseases.

   _____

7. America: love it or leave it.

   _____

8. I couldn't understand that one lecture, so I know that this course will be impossible.

   _____

9. If we pass laws against fully-automatic weapons, then it won't be long before we pass laws on all weapons, then we will begin to restrict other rights, and finally, we will end up living in a communist state. Thus, we should not ban fully automatic weapons.

   _____

10. Since I'm not lying, it follows that I'm telling the truth.

    _____

11. A plane is a carpenter's tool, and a Boeing 737 is a plane, therefore the Boeing 737 is a carpenter's tool.

    _____

12. You say I shouldn't drink, but you haven't been sober for more than a year.

_____

13. We've got to stop them from banning pornography. Once they start banning one form of literature, they will never stop. Next thing you know, they will be burning all the books!

_____

14. In regard to my recent indictment for corruption, let's talk about what's really important instead—terrorists are out there, and if we don't stop them we're all gonna die!

_____

15. "I know tax increases are a bad idea," said the politician. "I pay taxes also, just like everyone else. I have a dog named Fido and I drive a minivan. I like to shop at Food Lion and eat at Hardee's every morning."

_____

16. Sam is riding her bike in her town in Maine, minding her own business. A station wagon comes up behind her and the driver starts beeping his horn and then tries to force her off the road. As he goes by, the driver yells "Get on the sidewalk where you belong." Sam sees that the car has Ohio plates and concludes that all Ohio drivers are jerks.

_____

17. Of course this mode of government is the best. We have had this government for over 200 years and no one has talked about changing it in all that time. So, it has got to be good.

_____

18. Ladies and gentlemen of the jury, look at the bloody clothes, the murder weapon. Imagine the helpless screams of the victim. Such a crime deserves no verdict except guilty, guilty!

_____

19. I'm not a doctor, but I play a doctor on TV, and I wouldn't dream of using anything but Tylenol for my toughest headaches.

_____

20. There are more laws on the books than ever before, and more crimes are being committed than ever before. Therefore, to reduce crime, we must eliminate the laws.

_____

Name: _____

**Remarks By The President Announcing The Beginning Of Military Action In Iraq**

Text of President Bush's remarks delivered Wednesday night, March 19, 2003, announcing the beginning of

U.S. led military action in Iraq.

**Fill in the *Jus Ad Bellum* or *Jus In Bello* condition that matches the statement.**

My fellow citizens, at this hour, American and coalition forces are in the early stages of military operations to

disarm Iraq, to free its people and to defend the world from grave danger._____


On my orders, coalition forces have begun striking selected targets of military importance

_____ to undermine Saddam Hussein's ability to wage war. These are opening stages of what

will be a broad and concerted campaign.


More than 35 countries are giving crucial support -- from the use of naval and air bases, to help with

intelligence and logistics, to the deployment of combat units. Every nation in this coalition has chosen to bear

the duty and share the honor of serving in our common defense. _____


To all the men and women of the United States Armed Forces now in the Middle East, the peace of a troubled

world and the hopes of an oppressed people _____ now depend on you.


That trust is well placed. _____


The enemies you confront will come to know your skill and bravery. The people you liberate

_____ will witness the honorable and decent spirit _____ of the American

military.


In this conflict, America faces an enemy who has no regard for conventions of war or rules of morality. Saddam

Hussein has placed Iraqi troops and equipment in civilian areas, attempting to use innocent men, women and

children as shields for his own military _____ -- a final atrocity against his people.


I want Americans and all the world to know that coalition forces will make every effort to spare innocent

civilians from harm. _____ A campaign on the harsh terrain of a nation as large as California could be longer and more difficult than some predict. _____ And helping Iraqis achieve a united, stable and free country _____ will require our sustained commitment.

We come to Iraq with respect for its citizens, for their great civilization and for the religious faiths they practice. _____ We have no ambition in Iraq, except to remove a threat and restore control of that country to its own people. _____

I know that the families of our military are praying that all those who serve will return safely and soon. Millions of Americans are praying with you for the safety of your loved ones and for the protection of the innocent. _____

For your sacrifice, you have the gratitude and respect of the American people. And you can know that our forces will be coming home as soon as their work is done.

Our nation enters this conflict reluctantly _____ yet, our purpose is sure. _____ The people of the United States and our friends and allies will not live at the mercy of an outlaw regime that threatens the peace with weapons of mass murder. _____

We will meet that threat now, with our Army, Air Force, Navy, Coast Guard and Marines, so that we do not have to meet it later with armies of fire fighters and police and doctors on the streets of our cities.

_____

Now that conflict has come, the only way to limit its duration _____ is to apply decisive force. _____ And I assure you, this will not be a campaign of half measures, _____ and we will accept no outcome but victory.

My fellow citizens, the dangers to our country and the world will be overcome. _____ We will pass through this time of peril and carry on the work of peace. _____ We will defend our freedom. _____ We will bring freedom to others and we will prevail. _____

May God bless our country and all who defend her. _____

# Chapter 1 Quiz

Name:_____

Matching: Match the vocabulary term to its definition
Each Item is worth 3 points

1) _____ Divine Command
2) _____ Normative Ethics
3) _____ Ethical Subjectivism
4) _____ Metaphysics
5) _____ Virtue Ethics
6) _____ Descriptive Ethics
7) _____ Emotivism
8) _____ Ethics
9) _____ Cultural Relativism
10) _____ Metaethics
11) _____ Morality

a) Branch of philosophy concerned with the study of the nature of reality, including what it means to be human

b) There are no moral truths and moral standards are neither true nor false but simply expressions or outbursts of feelings

c) Is concerned with appraising the logical foundations and internal consistencies of ethical systems

d) Gives us practical guidelines or behavioral norms

e) What is moral is relative to God, there are no universal moral principles that are binding on all people, morality is dependent on God's will and may differ from person to person or from religion to religion

f) Refers to the actual content of right and wrong

g) Refers to the process of determining right and wrong

h) Aims to discover and describe the moral belief of a given society

i) Focuses on the virtues produced in individuals and not the morality of specific acts

j) Moral right and wrong are relative to the individual person, it is a matter of individual opinion

k) Morality is created collectively by groups of humans and it differs from society to society

Multiple Choice and True False: Circle the correct answer.
Each item is worth 3 points.

12) Which metaethical side states that morality is different for different people?

    a) Cultural Relativism

    b) Relativist

    c) Ethical Egoism

    d) Universalist

13) Which category of moral actions states that acts are either mandated or prohibited?
    a) Morally obligatory
    b) Morally permissible
    c) Morally supererogatory

14) In universalist theories, morality is created rather than discovered
    a) True
    b) False

15) What are the two traditional subdivisions of moral philosophy?
    a) Divine command theory and natural law theory
    b) Normative ethics and metaethics
    c) Subjectivism and cultural relativism
    d) Metaphysics and metaethics

16) What is the funny phrase surrounding the making of excuses, especially as it relates to our environment?
    a) Snickers Defense
    b) Twinkie Defense
    c) Oreo Defense
    d) Krispy Kreme Defense

17) Which category of moral actions states that acts go beyond the call of duty?
    a) Morally obligatory
    b) Morally supererogatory
    c) Morally permissible

18) Which metaethical side states that moral truths exist that are true for all humans, regardless of their personal beliefs?
    a) Virtue Ethics
    b) Relativist
    c) Ethical Egoism
    d) Universalist

19) Metaphysical materialism supports the idea that morality is based on our biological drives.
    a) True
    b) False

20) Who said "The unexamined life is not worth living"?
    a) Plato
    b) Pascal
    c) Socrates
    d) Aristotle

21) Metaphysical dualism deals with the idea that our bodies are made up of two parts.
    a) True
    b) False

22) Which category of moral actions states that acts are neither mandated nor forbidden?
    a) Morally supererogatory
    b) Morally permissible
    c) Morally obligatory

23) Which of the following is **NOT** one of the parts of morality?
    a) Internal
    b) Group consideration
    c) External
    d) Serving proper goals

24) Who said, "The heart has its reasons which reason knows nothing of."
    a) Kierkegaard
    b) Pascal
    c) Plato
    d) Descartes

25) Which of the following is an example of a noncognitive ethical theory?
    a) Universalist theories
    b) Epistemology
    c) Emotivism
    d) Ethical relativism

26) According to class discussion, the terms "ethics" and "morality" can be used interchangeably.
    a) True
    b) False

27) Which category of ethical norms was used by Adolf Hitler in his writing of the *Mein Kampf* to justify the killing of the Jews?
    a) Generalism
    b) Antinomianism
    c) Non-Conflicting Moral Norms
    d) Graded Absolutism

28) In determinism, there is free will.
    a) True
    b) False

Short Answer: Each question must be answered in complete sentences. Please type answers and attach to quiz.
Each item is worth 8 points.

| Essay Grading Rubric | | | | |
| --- | --- | --- | --- | --- |
| Excellent | Proficient | Competent | Basic | Novice |
| 100%--8 Points | 75%--6 Points | 50%--4 Points | 25%--2 Points | 0%--0 Points |
| Answered question correctly and provided answer in complete sentences. | Answer to the question was partially correct. OR Answered question correctly, but did not provide answer in complete sentences. | Answer was either missing information OR did not provide enough explanation to answer. | Answer provided gave a little correct information. | Did not answer question OR answer provided was incorrect. |

29) What are the six categories given in class that help define the nature of ethical norms? **Give detailed information about each category.**

30) Do all actions have a moral dimension? If not, why do some actions involve moral judgments while others are morally neutral? **Explain using specific examples.**

# Chapter 2 Quiz

Name:_____

Multiple Choice & True/False:
3 Points each

1) At which level of critical thinking would you try to make sense of the world around us?
   a) Interpretation
   b) Experience
   c) Praxis
   d) Analysis

2) Where does resistance belong in relation to the 3-tiered approach to critical thinking?
   a) At the end of interpretation
   b) At the end of experience
   c) At the beginning of analysis
   d) At the beginning of interpretation

3) What is the most common type of evidence that we might use in research?
   a) Survey
   b) Expert Opinion
   c) Eyewitness Testimony
   d) Personal Experience

4) Prescriptive statements deal with what ought to be in nonmoral values.
   a) True
   b) False

5) Descriptive statements are just about the facts.
   a) True
   b) False

6) Ethics primarily deals with descriptive statements with prescriptive being in a supporting role.
   a) True
   b) False

7) At which level of critical thinking would you look at your experience and interpretation?
   a) Interpretation
   b) Experience
   c) Praxis
   d) Analysis

8) Which of the following statements would you hear from some someone who is engaged in doublethink?

    a) Do unto others as you would have them do unto you.

    b) I agree with both sides of the argument.

    c) I'll have to rethink this now that you've brought up a new point.

    d) The ends justify the means.

9) At which level of critical thinking would you consider all that you have been a part of?

    a) Praxis

    b) Analysis

    c) Interpretation

    d) Experience

10) "I don't see a problem" is what type of defense mechanism?

    a) I'm struggling

    b) Cliches

    c) Doublethink

    d) Denial

11) Holding two contradictory views at the same time is what type of distraction?

    a) Coping

    b) Doublethink

    c) Superficial Tolerance

    d) I'm struggling

12) In constructing a moral argument, we should begin by

    a) Engaging in rhetoric

    b) Coming up with a conclusion

    c) Checking for fallacies

    d) Compiling a list of premises

13) Which type of defense mechanism would be not wanting to learn about something because one does not want to?

    a) Anger

    b) Ignorance

    c) Distraction

    d) Coping

14) Opinions are?

    a) Most likely to be found at the level of moral analysis

    b) The foundation of moral thinking and ought to be respected

    c) Based on feeling rather than on reason

    d) Never True

15) Which type of defense mechanism allows us to work through challenges to our worldview while maintaining our integrity?

   a) Resistance

   b) Anger

   c) I'm struggling

   d) Coping

16) In resolving a moral dilemma, we should first?

   a) Get our facts straight

   b) Make a list of all the alternative courses of action

   c) Make a list of the moral duties and values involved

   d) Come up with a possible solution

Identify which statement in each question is the conclusion:
3 Points each

17) Identify which statement in each question is the conclusion: [1] We have an obligation to become the best person we can. [2] One of the primary purposes of education is to make us better people. [3] Colleges should seriously consider having a community service requirement for graduation. [4] Community service has been shown to increase students' self-esteem and facilitate their moral development.

   a) 1

   b) 2

   c) 3

   d) 4

18) Identify which statement in each question is the conclusion: [1] Racism and sexism are wrong, [2] because all people deserve equal respect.

   a) 1

   b) 2

19) Identify which statement in each question is the conclusion: [1] It is immoral to use rabbits in cosmetic experiments, [2] causing pain is immoral and [3] animals such as rabbits are capable of feeling pain.

   a) 1

   b) 2

   c) 3

20) Identify which statement in each question is the conclusion: [1] People need to pass a driving test to get a license to drive a car. [2] People should also have to take a test and get a license before they can become a parent. [3] Parenting is a greater responsibility and requires more skill than driving.

   a) 1

   b) 2

   c) 3

21) Identify which statement in each question is the conclusion: [1] Embryos are not persons with moral rights. [2] Furthermore, the embryos used in stem cell research are going to be discarded anyway. [3] We have a moral obligation to help people suffering from disease and the use of stem cell research has the potential to help many of these people, [4] stem cell research should be legal.

   a) 1
   b) 2
   c) 3
   d) 4

Match the fallacy with the statement:
**Each fallacy can be used only once**
3 Points each

22) _____ We've got to stop them from banning pornography. Once they start banning one form of literature, they will never stop. Next thing you know, they will be burning all the books.

23) _____ In regard to my recent indictment for corruption, let's talk about what's really important instead...terrorists are out there, and if we don't stop them we're all gonna die!

24) _____ Of course this mode of government is the best. We have had this government for over 200 years and no one has talked about changing it in all this time.

25) _____ I know tax increases are a bad idea...I pay taxes also, just like everyone else. I have a dog named Fido and I drive a minivan. I like to shop at Food Lion and eat at Hardee's every morning.

26) _____ Capital Punishment is morally acceptable because murderers should be put to death.

27) _____ Catherine Zeta Jones says to use T-Mobile because that phone company is the best.

28) _____ Oh, hi mom. … The Arctic expedition was a remarkable success, I'm all but certain there's a Nobel Prize in my future. Actually, I shouldn't say that. I'm entirely certain. No, mother, I could not feel your church group praying for my

a) Appeal to tradition
b) Ignorance
c) Begging the question
d) Plain Folks
e) False Clause
f) Slippery Slope
g) Red Herring
h) Non-Sequitur
i) Abusive Fallacy
j) Hasty generalization
k) Appeal to Authority
l) Fallacy of Equivocation

safety. The fact that I'm home safe is not proof that it worked. No, I'm not sassing you in Eskimo talk.

29) _____ I support the oil sanctions Obama and the European Union placed on Iran. After all, Iran has not proven that they aren't in the process of enriching uranium for nuclear weapons

30) _____ My parents used to get into arguments all the time and they ended up getting divorced. Logic teaches people how to make arguments. Therefore, if you want a happy marriage, you should stay away from logic

31) _____ I'm not surprised you're arguing that hate speech should not be banned on college campuses. After all, you're one of the most hateful, racist, and insensitive people I've ever met.

32) _____ If we can land on the Moon and Mars, then we can cure all diseases

33) _____ I support racial profiling and the questioning of all Arabs by security officers in airports. Remember, it was Arabs who blew up the Twin Towers.

The following question is worth 1 point:

34) Who were they trying to burn in the video clip?

    a) A Duck

    b) A Piece of wood

    c) A Hamburger

    d) A Witch

# Chapter 3 Quiz

Name:_____

Matching: Match the vocabulary term to its definition
Each question is worth 3 points

1) _____ Moral Sentiments
2) _____ Determinism
3) _____ Moral Motivation
4) _____ Moral Indignation
5) _____ Sympathy
6) _____ Conscience
7) _____ Altruistic Behavior
8) _____ Moral Character
9) _____ Guilt
10) _____ Moral Outrage
11) _____ Moral Sensitivity
12) _____ Moral Responsibility
13) _____ Moral Reasoning

a) Feeling that arises when we violate a moral norm

b) Happens when we witness a violation or transgression of the boundaries of moral decency

c) An inner sense of right and wrong

d) The placing of moral values above nonmoral values

e) The awareness of how our actions affect others

f) The application of logical analysis to moral issues

g) Is the anger we feel at the sight of others being harmed

h) The capacity for and inclination to imagine the feelings of others

i) The belief in or practice of disinterested and selfless concern for the well-being of others

j) The status of morally deserving praise, blame, reward, or punishment for an act or omission, in accordance with one's moral obligations

k) The integration of moral reasoning, moral sensitivity, and morel motivation into one's personality

l) Are emotions that move us to feel moral approval or disapproval

m) Says there is no such thing as conscious moral direction, we are the product of our environment or genetic inheritance

Multiple Choice and True/False: Circle the correct answer.
Each question is worth 3 points.

14) Which of the following questions would you be most likely to hear from someone, in both Kohlberg's and Gilligan's preconventional stage of moral reasoning, when they are confronted with a moral issue?

    a) "Will you accept responsibility?"

    b) "What's in it for me?"

    c) "Is this going to harm anyone?"

    d) "What will others think?"

15) What did Plato suggest for those whose souls are incurably evil?
    a) Jail
    b) Torture
    c) Execution
    d) Time-out

16) Moral knowledge is also known as what?
    a) Metaphysics
    b) Metaethics
    c) Epistemology
    d) Normative Ethics

17) Plato defined conscience as an activity of the soul that directs us toward the good.
    a) True
    b) False

18) Conscience is broken into two parts: cognitive and defective
    a) True
    b) False

19) Psychoanalyst Sigmund Freud identified the conscience with the?
    a) Superego
    b) Big ego
    c) Heart
    d) Ego

20) Which of the following factors would a cultural relativist argue is most important in the formation of our consciences?
    a) conscious moral direction
    b) environment
    c) intuition
    d) good genes

21) The study of ethics must not take into account relevant facts about human nature
    a) True
    b) False

22) Who said, "We must believe that conscience of man is not a product of nature?"
    a) Nietzsche
    b) Freud
    c) C.S. Lewis
    d) Plato

23) Which of the following questions would you be most likely to hear from
people in the postconventional stage of moral reasoning when they are
confronted with a moral issue in their lives?

a) "Will you accept responsibility for what happens?"

b) "Is someone going to be harmed by my action?"

c) "What's in it for me?"

d) "What will others think?"

24) Which of the following is not one of the three factors related to conscience

a) Biological factors

b) Environmental factors

c) Work skills

d) Heredity

Short Answer: Each question must be answered in complete sentences. Please type
answers and attach to quiz.
Each question is worth 14 points.

| Essay Grading | | | | |
|---|---|---|---|---|
| Exbelte | Proficie | Compete | Basi | Novic |
| 100%--14 | 75%--10.5 | 50%--7 | 25%--3.5 | 0%--0 |
| Answered question correctly and provided answer in complete sentences. | Answer to the question was partially correct. OR Answered question correctly, but did not provide answer in complete sentences. | Answer was either missing information OR did not provide enough explanation to answer. | Answer provided gave a little correct information. | Did not answer question OR answer provided was incorrect. |

25) Jesus taught that we should "turn the other cheek" and "love our enemies." Discuss
this in light of the following quote from Aristotle regarding the moral value of moral
indignation in the face of mistreatment. Aristotle said, "People who are not angered by
the right things, or in the right way, or at the right times, or towards the right people, all
seem to be foolish...Since he is not angered, he does not seem to be the sort to
defend himself and such willingness to accept insults to oneself or to overlook insults
to one's family and friends is slavish."
Do the teachings of Jesus prohibit resentment and indignation? Support your answer.
Hint: Look at pages 83-84 in your textbook.

26) Describe the six parts of Kohlberg's Stages of Moral Development. Be specific.

# Chapter 4 Quiz

Name:_____

Matching: Match the vocabulary term to its definition.
Each question is worth 4 points.

1) _____ Ethical Skepticism
2) _____ Tolerance
3) _____ Values Clarification
4) _____ Opinion
5) _____ Ethical Subjectivism
6) _____ Nihilism
7) _____ Emotivism

a) Based on nonjudgmental and nondirective discussion of moral issues
b) This has the idea of tolerance and respect for other's lifestyles
c) A statement that is based only on a feeling rather than on fact
d) It is impossible to know whether moral truths exist or the nature of these truths
e) A type of ethical relativism that claims that morality is relative to each individual person
f) Moral statements are neither true nor false but simply expressions of feeling
g) Believes that values are not real, people might have various moral beliefs but really nothing is good or bad or right or wrong

Multiple Choice and True/False: Circle the correct answer.
Each question is worth 4 points.

8) According to Ethical Subjectivism, there is a right and wrong.
    a) True
    b) False

9) In Emotivism, all moral statements are not meaningless.
    a) True
    b) False

10) In Ethical Subjectivism, individual opinions must provide the standard of moral truth.
    a) True
    b) False

11) In Emotivism, there are moral truths.
    a) True
    b) False

12) In Ethical Subjectivism moral statements are based on personal opinion.
    a) True
    b) False

13) In Ethical Subjectivism, morality is based on what?

    a) Culture

    b) Religion

    c) Books

    d) Opinion

14) Another way to look at tolerance is through which phrase?

    a) Live and let's get along.

    b) Live and let die.

    c) Live and let live.

    d) Live and let's love.

15) To the heart of Ethical Subjectivism, moral opinions are based solely on what?

    a) Fear

    b) Feelings

    c) Facts

    d) Ideas

16) Ethical Subjectivism is sometimes called what?

    a) Individual Choice

    b) Individual Idea

    c) Individual Thought

    d) Individual Relativism

17) In Ethical Subjectivism, we can know with certainty whether or not objective moral standards exist.

    a) True

    b) False

18) Ethical skepticism is closely related to the idea of what?

    a) Atheism

    b) Agnosticism

    c) Altruism

    d) Antinomianism

Short Answer: Each question must be answered in complete sentences. Please type answers and attach to quiz.
Each question is worth 14 points

| Essay Grading Rubric | | | | |
|---|---|---|---|---|
| Excellent | Proficient | Competent | Basic | Novice |
| 100%--14 Points | 75%--10.5 Points | 50%--7 Points | 25%--3.5 Points | 0%--0 Points |
| Answered question correctly and provided answer in complete sentences. | Answer to the question was partially correct. OR Answered question correctly, but did not provide answer in complete sentences. | Answer was either missing information OR did not provide enough explanation to answer. | Answer provided gave a little correct information. | Did not answer question OR answer provided was incorrect. |

19) Are feelings alone a reliable moral guide?


20) Describe the four critiques of Ethical Subjectivism and explain each one.

# Chapter 5 Quiz

Name:_____

Matching: Match the vocabulary term to its definition
Each question is worth 4 points

1) _____ Religious
2) _____ Religion
3) _____ Divine Command
4) _____ Spirituality
5) _____ Natural Law
6) _____ Civil Religion

a) A set of beliefs about a transcendent God (god)
b) Morality is dependent on or relative to God's commands and therefore can change from time to time and person to person
c) Is a blend of religion and cultural relativism
d) Is the social aspect involving that institution of beliefs
e) Maintains that morality is universal and unchanging and that God commands something because it is right prior to the command
f) Is an inner attitude of reverence for the ultimate moral worth and belief in God

Multiple Choice and True/False: Circle the correct answer
Each question is worth 4 points

7) Morality is dependent on or relative to God and morality does exist independently of God's will.
   a) True
   b) False

8) Who said, "The heart has its reasons which reason does not know. . . . It is the heart which experiences God, and not the reason?"
   a) Emil Brunner
   b) C.S. Lewis
   c) Blaise Pascal
   d) Bertrand Russell

9) If there is no God then, according to divine command theory?
   a) each person should decide individually what is right or wrong for him or her
   b) morality would still exist
   c) there would be no morality
   d) morality would be relative to each culture

10) Which of the following is not considered part of the Divine Command Theory?
   a) Christianity
   b) Judaism
   c) Islam
   d) Buddhism

11) Which of the following is true according to divine command theory?
   a) It was morally acceptable for the terrorists to bomb the World Trade Center on 9/11, if the command to do so came from God.
   b) God would not command a person to commit an act of terror because it is morally wrong to target innocent people.
   c) The moral code embodied in the Ten Commandments is morally binding on all people, including atheists, at all times.
   d) God does not exist because an all-loving God is incompatible with the existence of evil in the world.

12) Divine command theory is a type of what?
   a) Ethical atheism
   b) Emotivist Theory
   c) Universal moral theory
   d) Ethical Relativism

13) Civil religion is a mix of Divine Command and Cultural Relativism.
   a) True
   b) False

Short Answer: Each question must be answered in complete sentences. Please type answers and attach to quiz.
Each question is worth 16 points.

14) What are the three claims of Divine Command? Explain each one.

15) What are the four statements that C.S. Lewis makes regarding religion and morality?

16) What are the three critiques of Divine Command? Explain each one.

# Chapter 6 Quiz

Name:_____

Multiple Choice and True/False: Circle the correct answer.
Each question is worth 5 points.

1) Cultural relativism is concerned with what?
    a) Needs to be
    b) Can be
    c) Ought to be
    d) Has to be

2) Which of the following is not a relative ethical theory?
    a) Ethical Subjectivism
    b) Divine Command
    c) Cultural Relativism
    d) Emotivism

3) Why did Nazi Adolf Eichmann argue at his trial that he had done nothing wrong?
    a) He did not break any laws of his country.
    b) He was being falsely accused of committing acts that he had not committed.
    c) He was coerced (lacked free will) into doing what he had done because his family would have been sent to prison or exterminated if he had not followed orders.
    d) He believed morality was a private choice.

4) Cultural Relativism does not work in what kind of society?
    a) Alien
    b) Pluralist
    c) Communist
    d) Conventional

5) Which of the following is most likely to follow as a result of adopting cultural relativism?
    a) Suspicion and distrust of the norms and values of different cultures.
    b) The disappearance of disagreement in a pluralist society regarding moral values.
    c) Respect and tolerance for the norms and values of different cultures.
    d) Greater acceptance of constructive criticism of one's own cultural norms.

6) Herodotus said that conceptions of right and wrong differ from culture to culture.
    a) True
    b) False

7) Cultural Relativists claim that it is arrogant to judge other cultures.
    a) True
    b) False

160

8) What event led to a general disillusionment with the theory of cultural relativism?
   a) United Nations
   b) Nazi Holocaust
   c) Increased use of fieldwork among anthropologists
   d) Development of Social Darwinism

9) Who said, "We recognize that morality differs in every society, and is a convenient term for socially approved habits?"
   a) Barack Obama
   b) Ibn Khaldun
   c) Ruth Benedict
   d) Jean-Jacques Rousseau

10) Cultural Relativism is a universalist theory.
   a) True
   b) False

11) Which of the following is not one of the claims made by cultural relativists?
   a) It is arrogant for us to judge other cultures.  We should always be tolerant of them.
   b) The moral code of our own society has no special status, it is but one among many.
   c) There is no objective standard that can be used to judge one's society's code as better than another's.  There are no moral truths that hold for all people at all times.
   d) Different societies do not have different moral codes.

12) Cultural relativism confuses morality with what?
   a) Ways of life
   b) Custom
   c) Thoughts
   d) Rituals

13) Cultural relativism is the same as cultural diversity.
   a) True
   b) False

14) People act more morally when others are around.
   a) True
   b) False

15) Cultural relativism can be viewed as nothing more than socially disapproved customs.
   a) True
   b) False

16) Which answer best fits the following statement, "Simply the observation that there are disagreements among cultures regarding moral behavior?"
  a) Cultural Relativism
  b) Sociological Relativism
  c) Pluralism
  d) Darwinism

17) Cultural relativism does not correctly describe how we make moral judgments.
  a) True
  b) False

18) Cultural Relativism is logical.
  a) True
  b) False

19) Cultural relativism says that public opinion determines right and wrong.
  a) True
  b) False

20) Cultural Relativism creates a divisive mentality.
  a) True
  b) False

Short Answer: Answer in complete sentences.
Each question is worth 0 points.

21) What are the seven critiques of Cultural Relativism? Describe each one.
  This question will not be counted on your quiz, but it might appear on your exam so you will want to know the answer!!!!
  I'm just sayin'.

# Chapter 7 and Abortion Quiz

Name:_____

Matching: Match the vocabulary term to its definition.
Each question is worth 2 points.

1) _____ Beneficence
2) _____ Viability
3) _____ Fetus
4) _____ Spontaneous Abortions
5) _____ Elective Abortions
6) _____ Therapeutic Abortions
7) _____ Justice
8) _____ Zygote
9) _____ Autonomy
10) _____ Eugenic Abortions
11) _____ Induced Abortions
12) _____ Nonmaleficence
13) _____ Embryo

a) Done to maintain or save mother's life
b) Refers to the right to make decisions about one's own life and body without coercion by others
c) Occur naturally with no outside intervention, missed implants or miscarriage
d) Helping others on the grounds of compassion
e) Done because the fetus is known to be handicapped or at risk of being born with a handicap
f) Done strictly for parental "convenience"
g) Happens between 26-28 weeks when the fetus could survive outside the womb
h) Has both a social and political meaning; socially it means treating similar kinds of people similarly, politically it means that there is an allocation of scarce medical resources
i) Generated by outside intervention, these are abortions of pregnancies that will result in a live birth if left alone
j) "First, do not harm"
k) A cell or group of cells that results from the union of the sperm and egg
l) The developing human from the eighth week until birth
m) The developing human individual from the second through seventh week of pregnancy

Multiple Choice & True/False:
2 Points each

14) Ethical Subjectivism is concerned with the self-interests that are rational.
    a) True
    b) False

15) Which abortion technique was not discussed in class?
    a) Saline Injection
    b) Suction
    c) DNC
    d) Plan B

16) Psychological egoism makes a claim about human nature and the way things are.
   a) True
   b) False

17) Which abortion technique is usually performed most often in the first trimester?
   a) Saline
   b) Hysterotomy
   c) DNC
   d) Suction

18) Which court case shifted the focus of abortion regulation to the state level?
   a) Roe v. Wade
   b) Planned Parenthood vs. Danforth
   c) Doe v. Bolton
   d) Webster v. Reproductive Health Services

19) Which court case prohibited states from requiring a father's consent?
   a) Planned Parenthood vs. Danforth
   b) Webster v. Reproductive Health Services
   c) Roe v. Wade
   d) Doe v. Bolton

20) Universal ethical egoism states that everyone should always act in his or her own best self interest?
   a) True
   b) False

21) Which of the following is not one of the key claims of ethical egoism?
   a) People achieve happiness by pursuing their rational self-interests
   b) People ought to pursue their rational self-interests
   c) Individual happiness is the greatest moral good
   d) Individuals should do what feels right

22) At which point, as discussed in class, does viability happen?
   a) 15-18 weeks
   b) 22-24 weeks
   c) 15-18 days
   d) 22-24 days

23) Which court case determined the mother's health in the abortion factor?
   a) Webster v. Reproductive Health Services
   b) Planned Parenthood vs. Danforth
   c) Roe v. Wade
   d) Doe v. Bolton

24) Which of the following is one the items that came out of Roe v. Wade?

      a) How long abortion procedures should take place

      b) Which states would allow abortions

      c) Dividing pregnancy into trimesters

      d) Which doctors can perform abortions

Short Answer: Each question must be answered in complete sentences. Please type answers and attach to quiz.
Each question is worth 14 points.

| Essay Grading Rubric | | | | |
|---|---|---|---|---|
| Excellent | Proficient | Competent | Basic | Novice |
| 100%--14 Points | 75%--10.5 Points | 50%--7 Points | 25%--3.5 Points | 0%--0 Points |
| Answered question correctly and provided answer in complete sentences. | Answer to the question was partially correct. OR Answered question correctly, but did not provide answer in complete sentences. | Answer was either missing information OR did not provide enough explanation to answer. | Answer provided gave a little correct information. | Did not answer question OR answer provided was incorrect. |

25) What are the arguments against abortion? Be specific.


26) Describe the difference between developmental view and essentialist view. Be specific.


27) What are the four arguments against ethical egoism? Explain each answer.


28) What are the arguments for abortion? Be specific.

# Chapter 9 Quiz

Name:_____

Multiple Choice and True/False: Circle the correct answer.
Each question is worth 5 points.

1) In Natural Law, morality is grounded in a changing moral law.
   a) True
   b) False

2) Which argument for the existence of God fits the following: God is the greatest being imaginable?
   a) Moral Law Argument
   b) Teleological
   c) Ontological
   d) Cosmological

3) In Natural Law, we can take refuge in the human laws or customs of their culture.
   a) True
   b) False

4) In Natural Law, morality is reason put into action.
   a) True
   b) False

5) Human Laws always come before Natural Laws.
   a) True
   b) False

6) Natural Law is a universal moral theory that applies to all people.
   a) True
   b) False

7) Natural Law is cosmological, that is it is grounded in a specific view of the purpose or goal of the natural order.
   a) True
   b) False

8) In Natural Law, human laws are only binding if they are just and consistent with Natural Law.
   a) True
   b) False

9) Which argument for the existence of God fits the following: There must be a Law giver?

    a) Teleological

    b) Cosmological

    c) Moral Law Argument

    d) Ontological

10) Which religious body has Natural Law at its center?

    a) Judaism

    b) Protestants

    c) Catholics

    d) Islam

11) Which of the following is **not** one of the key claims of Natural Law?

    a) Humans cannot access natural law through the use of reason.

    b) Manmade laws are authoritative only if they are just and consistent with the principles of Natural Law.

    c) Natural law is universal and applies to all humans at all times.

    d) Morality is found in unchanging principles of moral (natural)law in nature.

12) The basic principle in Natural Law is to what?

    a) Do good and evil.

    b) Do good and avoid evil.

    c) Do evil and avoid good.

    d) Do or do not. There is no try.

13) Which argument for the existence of God fits the following: The universe evidences a great design?

    a) Moral law argument

    b) Cosmological

    c) Teleological

    d) Ontological

14) Which of the following is not one of the four fundamental goods in Natural Law?

    a) Money

    b) Society

    c) Knowledge

    d) Life

15) Natural law requires a belief in God.

    a) True

    b) False

16) Which argument for the existence of God fits the following: The world could not exist on its own so there must have been a first cause?

    a) Ontological

    b) Cosmological

    c) Teleological

    d) Moral Law Argument

Short Answer: Each question must be answered in complete sentences. Please type answers and attach to quiz.

Each question is worth 10 points

| Essay Grading Rubric | | | | |
|---|---|---|---|---|
| Excellent | Proficient | Competent | Basic | Novice |
| 100%--10 Points | 75%--7.5 Points | 50%--5 Points | 25%--2.5 Points | 0%--0 Points |
| Answered question correctly and provided answer in complete sentences. | Answer to the question was partially correct. OR Answered question correctly, but did not provide answer in complete sentences. | Answer was either missing information OR did not provide enough explanation to answer. | Answer provided gave a little correct information. | Did not answer question OR answer provided was incorrect. |

17) What are the five critiques of Natural Law? Explain each one and be specific.

18) Describe civil disobedience and when civil disobedience can be used. Also, what is the criteria for civil disobedience? Make sure you answer both parts.

# Chapter 12 Quiz

Name:_____

Multiple Choice and True/False: Circle the correct answer.
Each question is worth 5 Points.

1) A virtue is the midpoint between the vice of excess and the vice of what?
   a) Disaster
   b) Destruction
   c) Deficiency
   d) Defeat

2) Virtue ethics is based on what?
   a) Wisdom
   b) Knowledge
   c) Attitude
   d) Character

3) For the Greeks virtue and reason are separate.
   a) True
   b) False

4) C.S. Lewis calls the poison of subjectivism in that we have replaced "I believe" with what?
   a) I Want
   b) I Have
   c) I Feel
   d) I Need

5) Virtue Ethics is an alternative ethical theory to right ethics.
   a) True
   b) False

6) Virtue Ethics is about right being over right action.
   a) True
   b) False

7) Morals are cultivated through habit.
   a) True
   b) False

8) Vice does not stand in our way of achieving happiness.
   a) True
   b) False

9) What is the Confucianism word for virtue?

    a) hen

    b) pen

    c) men

    d) jen

10) Who created the idea of the Doctrine of Mean?

    a) Lewis

    b) Augustine

    c) Plato

    d) Aristotle

11) Which of the following is not one of the natural virtues?

    a) Prudence

    b) Knowledge

    c) Justice

    d) Temperance

12) Augustine wrote Nicomachean Ethics.

    a) True

    b) False

Short Answer: Each question must be answered in complete sentences. Please type answers and attach to quiz.

Each item is worth 20 points

| Essay Grading Rubric | | | | |
|---|---|---|---|---|
| Excellent | Proficient | Competent | Basic | Novice |
| 100%--20 Points | 75%--15 Points | 50%--10 Points | 25%--5 Points | 0%--0 Points |
| Answered question correctly and provided answer in complete sentences. | Answer to the question was partially correct. OR Answered question correctly, but did not provide answer in complete sentences. | Answer was either missing information OR did not provide enough explanation to answer. | Answer provided gave a little correct information. | Did not answer question OR answer provided was incorrect. |

13) What are the six advantages to Virtue Ethics? Discuss each one.

14) Give 5 virtue characteristics that you try to exhibit in your life. Explain each one using examples.

# Just War and Capital Punishment Quiz

Name:_____

Questions below are based on notes and class discussion from Just War Theory. Each question is worth 4 points.

1) *Jus ad bellum* is about the conditions that should be met before going to war.
   - a) True
   - b) False

2) *Jus in bello* is the condition that should be met after war has ended.
   - a) True
   - b) False

3) A crusade is an effort of war to put evil against good.
   - a) True
   - b) False

4) Which of the following is not one of the characteristics of Just War Theory?
   - a) Leaders have a responsibility to protect the weak.
   - b) Violence is kept to a minimum.
   - c) Surrender is possible and desired.
   - d) That evil cannot and should not be restrained.

5) Pacifism is the denial of moral justification for the use of deadly force.
   - a) True
   - b) False

6) In a crusade, there is the opportunity to end in surrender.
   - a) True
   - b) False

7) Discrimination is described as the targeting of noncombatants.
   - a) True
   - b) False

8) In which book, written by that famous Thomas, is found the basic outline of the Just War Theory?
   - a) Summa Cum Laude
   - b) Summa Summa
   - c) Summa Wrestler
   - d) Summa Theologica

9) Which type of pacifism is closely associated with military service?
   a) Satyapraha
   b) Absolute Pacifists
   c) Conscientious Objection
   d) Ahimsa

10) Which of the following is not one of the types of pacifism discussed in class?
   a) Conscientious Objection
   b) Absolute Pacifists
   c) Ahimsa
   d) Satyapraha

11) Which person is closely associated with Satyapraha?
   a) Obama
   b) Plato
   c) Yoda
   d) Gandhi

12) Which person is closely associated with the Just War Theory?
   a) Thomas Edison
   b) Thomas Jefferson
   c) Thomas Paine
   d) Thomas Aquinas

13) This condition in *Jus ad bellum* requires that a legitimate authority declare war?
   a) Right Intent
   b) Right Spirit
   c) Last Resort
   d) Competent Authority

14) A jihad is a type of crusade.
   a) True
   b) False

15) An absolute pacifist believes that all violence is wrong, even in self-defense.
   a) True
   b) False

Questions below are based on notes and class discussion on Capital Punishment. Each question is worth 4 points.

16) How many countries in the world currently have capital punishment in law and practice?
   a) 56
   b) 37
   c) 7
   d) 102

17) Which of the following is not one of the arguments made against capital punishment?
   a) The way in which the death penalty is administered.
   b) Reform becomes impossible.
   c) Death sentences are usually accompanied by long and inexpensive appeals.
   d) Mistakes are inevitable and irreversible.

18) Lex talionis is about a forward looking approach.
   a) True
   b) False

19) An abolitionist is in favor of abolishing the death penalty.
   a) True
   b) False

20) Capital Punishment is the infliction of death by the state as punishment for a crime.
   a) True
   b) False

21) Which of the following is not one of the arguments made against capital punishment?
   a) The way in which the death penalty is administered.
   b) Capital punishment is not cruel and unusual punishment.
   c) The demand for "justice" is inconsistent with forgiveness and redemption.
   d) The death penalty undermines the dignity of persons.

22) Which of the following is not one of the arguments made for capital punishment?
   a) Capital punishment expresses an appropriate demand for justice in society.
   b) Capital punishment is not cruel and unusual punishment.
   c) The cost of a life term is something society should have to bear.
   d) Capital punishment provides a unique deterrent against crime.

23) Which of the following is not part of a forward justification of punishment?
   a) Deterrence
   b) Retribution
   c) Reconciliation
   d) Rehabilitation

24) Procedural Abolitionists argue that there is something wrong with the death penalty in principle.
   a) True
   b) False

25) Which country in the world ranks 1st in state executions?
   a) Iran
   b) United States
   c) Canada
   d) China

# Euthanasia and Stem Cell Quiz

Name:_____

Questions below are based on notes and class discussion from Stem Cell Research.
Each question is worth 4 points.

1) Which of the following is not one of the sources, as discussed in class, listed as a location for adult stem cells?
   a) Body fat
   b) Liver
   c) Finger nails
   d) Skin

2) Which type of stem cell fits the following definition: These are cells that "can become almost anything." These may also be called "embryonic" stem cells because they come from cells that have started to differentiate in the second stage of early development called a "blastocyst"?
   a) Pluripotent
   b) Unipotent
   c) Totipotent
   d) Multipotent

3) Adult stem cells are cells that are fully grown.
   a) True
   b) False

4) Which type of stem cell fits the following definition: These are cells that "can become anything." They are also called "conceptual" stem cells because they only exist at the point "conception" and initial cell division?
   a) Multipotent
   b) Unipotent
   c) Totipotent
   d) Pluripotent

5) Embryonic Stem Cells must be taken at the blastocyst stage 5-6 weeks after fertilization.
   a) True
   b) False

6) Which type of stem cell fits the following definition: These cells that "become different things but only within a very limited range." These cells come from life developing in the womb after the "blastocyst" stage. They are called "adult" stem cells because they have already become so specifically coded and they can only become one of two or three different things and nothing else.?

    a) Multipotent

    b) Totipotent

    c) Unipotent

    d) Pluripotent

7) Which type of stem cell fits the following definition: These are cells that "can only become one thing." They are stem cells in the sense of being available to "replace" other damaged cells. But, all genetic codes in these cells have been turned off except for one?

    a) Pluripotent

    b) Unipotent

    c) Totipotent

    d) Multipotent

8) There are two categories of stem cells.

    a) True

    b) False

Questions below are based on notes and class discussion on Physician Assisted Suicide. Each question is worth 4 points.

9) Which of the following is not one of the arguments used against euthanasia?

    a) Developmental view of personhood

    b) Unique value of human life

    c) Risk of slippery slope

    d) Medical concerns

10) Euthanasia means what?

    a) Good & Disease

    b) Good & Death

    c) Good & Destroyed

    d) Good & Dying

11) Which of the following is not one of the criteria for using Physician Assisted Suicide?

    a) Must make two verbal requests at least 15 days apart.

    b) Doctor must inform that the patient can rescind the request.

    c) Must be over 18.

    d) Diagnosed with any disease that will result in death in the next year.

12) Taking a direct action to terminate a patient's life because they have requested it is called mercy killing.
   a) True
   b) False

13) Which action of euthanasia would fit the following: Withholding life support or medical treatment at the patient's direct request or indirectly through a living will?
   a) Passive Involuntary
   b) Active Voluntary
   c) Passive Voluntary
   d) Active Involuntary

14) Advanced directives are sometimes also called Durable Power of Attorney.
   a) True
   b) False

15) Which of the following is not one of the criteria for irreversible brain damage?
   a) Unreceptive and unresponsiveness
   b) No spontaneous movements
   c) A Flat EEG
   d) Reflexes

16) Which action of euthanasia would fit the following: Physician-assisted suicide; administering a lethal injection or lethal dose at a patient's request?
   a) Passive Involuntary
   b) Active Voluntary
   c) Passive Voluntary
   d) Active Involuntary

17) Which action of euthanasia would fit the following: Giving an incompetent person, such as an infant or person in a coma, a lethal injection?
   a) Active Voluntary
   b) Passive Voluntary
   c) Passive Involuntary
   d) Active Involuntary

18) Which of the following is not one of the arguments in favor of euthanasia?
   a) Practical limitations
   b) Essentialist view of personhood
   c) Moral autonomy
   d) Quality of life

19) Which action of euthanasia would fit the following: Withholding life support or medical treatment from an incompetent person?

    a) Active Voluntary

    b) Passive Voluntary

    c) Active Involuntary

    d) Passive Involuntary

20) The primary role of hospice is to provide pain relief and comfort to the dying.

    a) True

    b) False

# Bibliography and References

Boss, Judith. *Ethics for Life: a Text with Readings*. 6th Edition. New York: McGraw-Hill Education. 2013. Print.

Commonwealth Law Revision Commission. http://www.cnmilaw.org/pdf/cmc_section/T1/26005.pdf. (accessed May 26, 2017).

"Death Row U.S.A" NAACP Legal Defense Fund. July 1, 2016. http://www.naacpldf.org/files/publications/DRUSA_Summer_2016.pdf

Gordon, Doris. "Abortion and Rights: Applying Libertarian Principles Correctly." *The International Journal of Sociology and Social Policy* 19, no. 3 (1999): 96-126.

Jeffrey, Terence. "AG Nominee Defending Partial-Birth Abortion: 'The Phrase "Living Fetus"' is 'Hopelessly Vague'." http://www.cnsnews.com/news/article/terence-p-jeffrey/ag-nominee-defending-partial-birth-abortion-phrase-living-fetus. (accessed May 26, 2017)

Partial-Birth Abortion: Recent Developments in the Law. http://congressionalresearch.com/RL30415/document.php?study=Partial-Birth+Abortion+Recent+Developments+in+the+Law. (accessed May 26, 2017).

"Turabian Style Citation." Coates Library. Trinity University. http://lib.trinity.edu/research/citing/Turabian_Notes_Citations.pdf

Made in the USA
Columbia, SC
24 August 2022

65946876R00107